1

MW01518195

Friend

an autobiography

By

Thomas Wermuth

*This book is dedicated to
the healing of the
Children of this world
young and old alike*

Table of Contents

Prelude

So often I get asked how I began studying the violin. Just recently I was asked *why* I began studying the violin. Wow. Why. That was actually a shock that I am still adjusting to. Why did I start learning the violin? For a while I really couldn't answer. But then one day, during an energy session I was having with a client that had been with me for many years, I started talking about it from a place that wasn't necessarily a usual place for me. I started channeling, and several hours later I had some answers that not only made sense, but filled in a large part of my life puzzle. That was in March of 2020, just a week before all hell broke loose and we were in for the ride of our lives. The Covid 19 Pandemic. And I've had a lot of time to process all of this, about a year and a half.

How I began the violin had been really easy to tell, and I always loved telling the story. It's a pretty classic story. I found a violin in my grandmother's attic.

You "found" a violin   hmmm

i always love playing in the attic   there is something magical about it   and it's scary too   i don't like going all the way up there by myself   where's daddy

1

Fast forwarding about sixty some years, I have spent my life devoted to the violin, to teaching the violin. The sound of the violin fascinates me to no end. I can sit for hours just making sound and finding out how it really works. I've loved playing and have dedicated the past forty some years to teaching children to play, as well as working with teachers to hone their own skills. When I am working with those teachers in some of my courses, my goal is to focus on the topics and boil down those topics that are the most important to talk about. After all of these years of teaching I think I have at least figured this out, and I believe two very important things that keep coming to mind are, memory and timing.

i love it when mamma makes her vegetable soup   the smell reminds me of walking into Hazelwood Elementary School   but those mean boys scare me   i hate it

Just tell the story

Memory is a really interesting subject. There are so many types of memory...sound, sight, kinesthetic, muscle, brain, and the list just keeps growing. Every student is different, we all know that, and if there is someone who disagrees, change vocations, please. The depth of 'memory' that is needed to play any instrument goes beyond ever being able to explain it. It goes right into our own very soul. If you, as a performer, are not willing to go those depths, then you should find another vocation too. Please do not fall into the trap of "those who can't do, teach". You need to go into your own soul not only when you express yourselves when you play, you need to be able to go there with your students. Otherwise, they will never be able to go there themselves.

Timing is also important, and I am not talking about rhythm at all. Of course rhythm is worked on from day one, no matter what method you might be using in your teaching but there is rarely a lesson that goes by when I always tell my students, "every note has a time and place in the universe to be placed, not too soon, and not too late".

Everything happens at the time it is supposed to   not too soon and not too late   timing is perfect   but very hard to trust

i have to hide my violin

Just tell your story Tom

9191919

mama i wet the bed again **youbigfuckingsissy**

It's okay Tom

you can't tell my secret Rankso it is my secret and i will never tell anyone
ever

Humiliated. I can't believe I am actually saying this out
loud. I don't think anyone knows this about me. This is one
of the most humiliating things anyone can ever experience.
If you have never experienced this as an ongoing issue, then
you have absolutely no idea how it feels. If you have, I know
how extraordinarily horrible it makes you feel. Horrible isn't
even the right word. Hideous is more like it. I am not sure
exactly when it started, I just know it lasted until about age
ten. Maybe I had been doing this all along since I was born
andyoustillthinkaboutiteverydayofyourlife

Dad was up at 4am every day except Sunday. That's the life
of a milkman. He worked for Model Farms Dairy, which then
changed to Meadow Gold and then Beatrice Foods. My dad
was a truly lovely man. I don't ever remember him staying
home from work. He was rarely sick when he was younger.
It wasn't until later that he began having heart problems. But
his ethics were so admirable.

4

i hate getting into bed with mama   i just hate it

noyoudontthatiswhyyouwetthebedanyway

But I am here for you   I am alway here

Mom would get up with dad and make a full breakfast for
him every day, then he would be out the door by half past
four. His day was long and hard. He wouldn't get home until
around 4:30 or 5 in the afternoon. I was always so happy to
see him. I used to wait until he pulled into the driveway and
I would often hide in his closet. His routine was to always
come in and change his clothes and I would jump out at him
and scare him. I'm not sure if he knew it was going to
happen, but he made the most out of it and I loved it. It's one
of my favorite memories with my dad.

but i still wet the bed most days   **whatashamehahaha**

It took many years for me to figure out that my bed wetting
would always happen after dad left for work. And I don't ever
recall it happening on a Sunday, or every six weeks when dad
would have his long weekend, which meant he was off from
after work on Friday until Sunday night. Oh, how he looked
forward to those long weekends off. But he was so good to
my mom. We would travel to Ohio on those weekends so she
could visit with her family. In the olden days it would take 3

5

1/2 hours to get there on back roads, not like the 2 hours once highways were built.

i promise to try harder mama

Everyone loved my dad. His customers on his two milk routes loved him, especially the elderly ladies. He had a ring of keys to everyone's house that needed him to put the milk order in the refrigerator. He would walk to the back doors and holler "milk...man" on the way so anyone would know he was coming. He was very good at a bit of flirting and would always take the time to ask how everyone was doing. On the rare days we had off school, I would go with him on the milk route. **youthoughtyouwereahelp...getoverit** He was always so grateful for me coming to "help", but I think I didn't actually make it any easier for him, and he never once complained or let me feel anything but his love. I learned all of the things about milk, how the cream rises to the top in the non-homogenized milk, how to put it correctly in the milk box outside by the back door, and how to tell the difference when it was just cream or half and half. I can tell the difference between large and small curd cottage cheese just by looking. And I also learned how to pee in an empty bottle in the back of the freezing truck. **atleastyoudidntpeeyourpants**

i love the familiar smell of the truck   just like at the dairy   milk

6

Dad would stand and drive the milk truck because it was quicker to get in and out and I stood on the passenger side and felt like such a big boy. I am sure, just by watching him, that is how I learned how to drive a stick shift. He had an A and a B route. I always hated the B route because he would have to deliver to a funeral home at about 5:30 am before the sun came up. I couldn't decide whether I would stay in the truck or go with him. Both ways scared me. And of course invariably he would hide and say "BOO" at me when I would go in with him. **hahahaha** Maybe he was just getting back at me for hiding in his clothes closet. "Ach mein glana Tommala" dad would say to me whenever I got scared or hurt. It means 'Oh my poor Tommy'.

daddy i love you so much

mama i'll just change my pajamas first

I would always hear dad talking to our pet parakeet, DeeDee, every morning when he got up. I think we went through at least three green and yellow DeeDee's, but he taught them all to say "hi" back to him. I remember hearing my mom yelling at my dad that he had to do something about my bed wetting, so he would get me up from bed before he left and take me to the bathroom and wait until I went. That is what eventually got me to stop. Funny how I am now seventy years old and when I get up during the night for the bathroom I always think of him.

i love you daddy

We lived in a very small house. Mom and dad paid $5,000 dollars for our home. Their monthly mortgage payment was fifty dollars. It is so hard, in 2022, to really wrap your brain around that. Originally it had two bedrooms, living room, kitchen, utility room, and a tiny bathroom. Mom was told she would never be able to give birth to children so I guess, back in the 1940's, it just didn't seem necessary to have a bigger house. There was a gravel driveway that came to the back door. Eventually the need came for a bit bigger living space, so the smaller bedroom turned into the dining room and a wall between the living room and the new dining room had an archway cut into it, and we had a room added onto the back of the house. Add to that , if you can imagine, they built a garage with a patio on the side. This happened sometime between 1952 and '53. Funny how I actually have memories of a few things then, including having a bad case of chicken pox at the age of 8 months.

mama   why do you always have to tell me that i cried non-stop for my first year

There was a reason Tom   Remember the darkness you felt after you were born   Darkness

Every time I had to leave my wet bed, usually just putting on clean underwear, and crawl into my mom and dad's bed, I felt horrible. I know most mornings I just cried silently lying there while she slept. I don't ever remember her comforting me. Of course, in the 1950's, that was just very taboo, to ever talk about it. Ever.

After I was born I remember my crib being in their bedroom. One time I pooped my diaper and dad was looking after me, and I decided to smear it all over the wall like finger-paint. When dad came in he started gagging and I remember laughing and laughing at him as he cleaned it up. Oh dad, I miss you so much these days.

but daddy there was darkness before this

We never got to have Christmas on the morning of December 25th because of dad's work. If it happened to fall on a Sunday then we would be at grandma's house in Ohio. We always celebrated on Christmas Eve. Dad would take me out to look at pretty lights, or to go to some store and waste time. I finally figured out something was up when we went to Taylor's Drug Store and he wanted to walk every aisle and look at things. I would hear him wherever he was because he whistled all the time. It drove my mom crazy. I think she was embarrassed by him. He hated shopping. When we would get home, Santa would have been there because the cookies and milk I left for him was gone, with a few crumbs left on the dish. On the rare times that we spent Christmas in Ohio, it always became a big ordeal because little Tommy wanted to open his presents on the 24th, but my grandma insisted that we would only do it on the morning of the 25th. I hated those arguments. **shedidntlikeyouanyway**

i can't choose mama   i can't choose   please don't make me

And with that I ran off to my room with my hands over my ears.

i'm not going to listen   i don't want to hear what they're saying

There were often terrible arguments in our household. Mom would often threaten divorce. She was awful to dad, often ridiculing him, telling him he wasn't good enough, that he never wanted to do anything or heaven forbid take a chance on anything, and of course he didn't make nearly the kind of money mom would have liked him to.

i hate it when you try and make me choose who i want to live with

My favorite times would be on Sundays when he would get home from church. We usually had a really nice breakfast. Most of the time mom was in a better mood. I would then sit on daddy's lap and he would talk to me softly, about what a good boy I was. Dad smoked cigars then and would take a match from the matchbook and just the cardboard end and slowly and softly rub it on my ear. It was hypnotizing. It seemed like we'd be there for hours. When I am tired these days I catch myself doing the same thing with my finger. I have even seen my daughter noticing that I do it. Such is love.

mama   why do you get mad at dad when i am on his lap   you always make me
go to my room

My favorite memory is of Mothers' Day when we would go to the Louisville amusement park, Fountaine Ferry. It was always pronounced fountain ferry. Ha. That's just like people trying to pronounce Louisville, Kentucky. It's pronounced Lou.a.Vul. Just don't move your lips and it works fine. I guess moving your lips is just way too much work for a true southerner to do.

daddy   tell me how we get there   please

On Sunday I would sit on his lap while mom and Carol cleaned up in the kitchen. We would go out the driveway, turn left down Rutland Avenue (there was only one way to go because back then our street was a dead end), right on Ashland and left on Southern Parkway, and from there we traveled to the west end of Louisville and about twenty minutes later we would get there. I could hardly sit still in the car. It cost ten cents back then to get in the park and mom got in free because it was Mothers' Day. What a hoot...mom hated the rides!

My dad would ask me what I was going to ride and of course we had to start with the Caterpillar and go from there. Every year I would stand and watch Carol go on the Comet,

11

that wonderful roller coaster, because she was old enough and I wasn't. I thought I would never get to ride it, but the day did come when I was finally old enough to ride. Dad went with me the first time. It was the best day ever! When the coaster ended they would let you pay a dime to stay on and ride again. We rode it 17 times in a row straight, and my dad finally begged me to get off. I think I could have stayed on forever. It was the freest I have ever felt in my life. It was a dream come true, finally.

Just like flying Tommy   just like flying

At some point during this time my dad's dad was beginning to have memory problems and his wife (my dad's mom had died well before I came along and he had remarried) wasn't able to cope with him, so my mom and dad opened our home to him. It was extremely difficult. I am aware now he was actually having advanced stage Altzheimers. He became nocturnal and would sleep most of the day and be up all night. I clearly remember one time in the middle of the night he came out of the bedroom thinking he was in a saloon and shooting his imaginary guns. For me it was frightening and intriguing at the same time. He slept in my bedroom and I slept on a cot in a small hallway right by the bathroom. It became increasingly difficult to the point that we finally had to put him in a nursing facility. He wasn't there for very long before he passed away. It was my first experience with death and funerals. I am just now remembering that it was in

January, and my mom as well as my dad also died in January.

Coincidence?

daddy   don't die   please don't die   i don't know what i'll do

When dad was 43 he had a massive heart attack. I'll never forget that night. Carol and I had already gone to bed. I think around 11pm Carol came and woke me up. Mom was getting dad in the car to go to the hospital.

you don't have to be so bossy to me   Carol

I remember my Uncle Jim came and got Carol and me and we went to their house.   It wasn't until the next afternoon when mom came to pick us up that we knew anything. I remember clearly asking mom "is daddy going to die?" Mom said she didn't know. I was surprised at how she looked. She looked mad. But, she always looked mad. This time she didn't look sad, just mad.

everthinkitwasyourfaultthathealmostdied

Dad began recovering, but back then he had to spend about three months in the hospital. Actually all of the doctors said they couldn't believe he survived. I overheard that one third of his heart had been damaged. But he didn't die.

i don't know what all this means   i don't know   i'm scared   and really sad

He couldn't die yet Tommy   He had to be there for you

13

I never got to see him in the hospital because kids weren't allowed. I missed him so much. When he finally got home he had to be in bed most of the time and had to rest for another three months. I would run home from school every day and sit on the bed with him. I think to this day that was my very favorite time with my dad. We talked about everything. And he always wanted to know how I was. I also remember several of my dad's friends from work coming by and giving us money. Dad often cried. Many years later I specifically remember a time when I knew how this all felt. Dad often felt like a failure because he was a "lowly" milkman, never graduated from high school and did very hard work for little money. One day when he was doing his yearly taxes I found him sitting at the dining room table with his head in his hands crying because he made such little money. I can clearly remember thinking I hoped I would never feel like this and that living a life I loved would help my dad's healing.

Time to confess   Tom

When I came out, at first it was to mom. I knew there was no other choice. By now I am in my mid thirties. It was one of the hardest things I could do. No matter what , though, I knew it would end up being okay. Something or someone was always looking over me. The only thing dad ever said was that he didn't really understand , but that he would always love me. **youfuckingfaggot**

14

I feel dad's energy often. When I am teaching sometimes I will say something and I'll look behind me and think, 'is that you dad?' My voice will even change abruptly and I will think I sounded like his voice. I can even feel his voice in me.

He will always be with you

Dad continued to have heart problems and heart surgeries. In June of 1991 he was sent home from the hospital not expecting to live more than a few weeks. I remember traveling around all summer teaching at various Suzuki institutes and carrying my black suit and calling home every day. I was on the road for about eight weeks. It was exhausting. But it just wasn't his time to leave yet.

Clearly there was a reason why

I went home for Thanksgiving that year, and mom had a story to tell. My dad was pretty much bed ridden by then and on oxygen. He was very weak and it was hard for him to talk. He mostly slept. But at some point shortly before mid November my dad's sister, my Aunt Agnes, showed us an old telegram dad had sent her. Apparently when my aunt and my uncle Jim got married, my dad was stationed as a medic in the South Pacific. The telegram read:

"Sorry I can't be at your wedding sis, but I promise to be there to dance with you at your fiftieth"
Aha

   When Christmas rolled around a month later, there was a big anniversary party planned for the day after, the 26th. It was their 50th anniversary. Dad had been in bed since at least September, but he started to rally, and we got him up, dressed, in a wheelchair, with his oxygen, into the car, and went to the celebration. It was amazing. My favorite memory of my dad was watching him actually stand at the bar and order a drink, and then truly dancing with his sister Agnes. We had a really great time. I don't think I had ever seen my dad so happy. Or mom either. Ever. Later we went home and dad went right to bed again. When I left a few days later to go back to Chicago, I knew it was the last time I would ever see him in this lifetime. Funny that I say this but many years later in Illinois I remember sitting in my family room and actually going into a trance and had a long conversation with him about Carol. When I came to about four hours had passed. I immediately went next door to my mom's and told her. I think it was the first time in many years that I even mentioned Carol to her. She was very intrigued and I knew she did not question what I told her at all.

Share the story

One day my aunt left me a message at the school to call home, so I knew immediately that he had passed. I talked to my mom and she was very calm and quiet, no drama, which surprised me a bit, but I also knew she was completely exhausted. I flew home the next day and mom met me at the airport. When we got home she showed me she had kept a diary of the last week, and it was so beautifully written. It seemed like she had stayed by dad's side every minute and what she wrote was very sweet. Dad had always been really afraid of dying, but that diary assured me that he went really happily and peacefully. Mom and I had our family visit that afternoon at the funeral home, which wasn't the easiest for me to do. My dad's family was there too.

The next morning was the first day of visitation. On our way out the door my mom grabbed a pale blue hat that my dad had worn every time he worked in his garden. He was known to never be out of the house without a hat on. When we would drive to Ohio to visit my mom's family he always wore a suit, tie and hat in the car. That's just the way everyone traveled in the 50's. When we got to the funeral home mom took the hat and put it under his hands and the smile on my mom's face was beautiful.

The day of the funeral I remember the first thing my mom said to me in the morning was that she didn't think she could do this. I told her I would be by her side and she hugged me tightly. We went to the gathering and mom wanted to be the last to leave so she could do her final moment with him. As I saw the casket being closed, I saw the blue hat and it made me feel very much at peace. It was January and we had a small service at the cemetery and then everyone was to come to our house for a gathering.

When we walked in the back door, my dad's blue hat was hanging in its usual spot by the door. I don't know if it was the state of being in shock about just everything but mom pointed to it and we both looked at each other and smiled. It stayed there until mom moved to Chicago about seven years later, when it came with her and resided by her back door until she left this lifetime.

And so it was

Lawrence John Wermuth   Lorney   Larry   Lonnie   Junie
9191919 - 171992
Nearly forty years with him   The lesson was   clearly Kindness

Snakebit

There once was a girl
Who had a little curl
Right in the middle of her forehead
And when she was good
She was very very good
And when she was bad
She was horrid

—1922   Baltimore Ohio

She was the seventh of eight children of Ida and Harry Gordon. Helen was first, then Bob, Ed, Dick, Ralph, and Maurice. After five boys in a row, Betty was the apple of her dad's eye. He doted on her, held her, and loved her so. That is until two years later when Jeannie came. Two years of feeling safe and secure and loved, after the five boys. Then all of a sudden she was no longer special, at least in her eyes. It took me many years to realize just how traumatic and horrible that must have been.

I never knew much about the younger years, not much until Betty was in high school. The reason why I knew a bit more about her life then was from her high school yearbook the year she graduated. There was a great love in her life. His name was Bud. It was obvious by the autographs and messages in the yearbook that they were going to be married.

One day when I was very young, in a fit of rage, Carol told me mom had been married and divorced before dad. I was devastated. **youpoorthing** She dragged me to dad's closet and pulled out the safety lock box, which was never locked to my knowledge, and there were all the divorce papers. The reason for the divorce, grounds of desertion. I learned many years later that he had a drinking problem and disappeared for a year. I guess another abandonment, this time from a man she obviously loved dearly.

no matter what anyone says i will always love you mama   no matter what

And no matter what you will always take care of her   That's what love is
And with that I promised Rankso and one of my life fates was sealed.

Mom's brother Maurice worked in Louisville Kentucky at the General Box company making corrugated boxes. One thing led to the next and my uncle introduced my dad to his sister Betty, and all I knew was they were married shortly after that. My dad was raised a very staunch Catholic. Mom didn't really care for that, so they were married outside of the church. At that time in life, probably the early 1940's, one was excommunicated from the Catholic Church if they dared marry outside of the church's permission. I know for many many years that was so very difficult for my dad. Oh, and to add to the challenges mom was already dealing with in her life, she was also told that she would never be able to bear children. I am not sure why she was told this or by whom. But later on in life mom realized how much my dad loved his church and faith, so she agreed to be remarried in the Catholic Church in a private ceremony, and I know it made dad feel really good. Interesting though that she never told me that until years later.

Miracles do happen Tom   every day

Some time around 1948 mom lost her favorite brother, Ralph. He was working on a bridge construction site and a crane swung around and crushed him against a cement wall and he died instantly. He left behind his wife, Beth, and three children, Kenneth, Carol and Susan. Beth was so devastated that she absolutely could not manage losing her husband and care for her three children. Kenneth and Susan were kept together and my mom and dad took Carol in. Of course this was to be a temporary solution.

I believe about six months went by and Beth seemed ready to have the children come back, but that only lasted for a few weeks. The situation went on and on for two years until my mom and dad went to court and legally adopted Carol.

My count is three   three abandonments   Jeannie's arrival   Bud vanishes   Ralph is gone

As time went on Carol began to feel safe and more loved. Until she was 6.

The Golden Boy arrives

it's really dark   Rankso

Tommy you have to really pay attention   You have much to accomplish   It's going to be really challenging   But isn't that what you signed up for?

it's really dark   i don't understand   is this what being born means Rankso and there is so much pain   it's almost like someone is trying to twist my head off   i didn't feel like this in my life before   i don't understand Rankso i am really scared

Right after I was taken home my mom ended up back in the hospital for blood transfusions. She was there for a few days. Since dad was spending time at the hospital my aunt Margaret was at home looking aft......

why is this hurting so much   mommy where are you   daddy   i don't know

who these two people are   Carol   who is Tommy   i am terrified   i think i am
going to go back where i just came from   this isn't right......
after me and Carol   why does Carol hate me so much to do this to me?

Everything happens for a reason Tom

I have always felt some level of discomfort when I see
pictures of myself in my first year. Mom was right. I did cry
all the time during that time.
youwerejustabigbabyallthetimeb...beaman   But I see such a
huge level of sadness in every single......every day i am scared   what
if she does it again   where is momma   dad where is mom   why does she ignore
me   what did i do   i'm sorry mama......
picture I see. Christmas. My family looking lovingly at me.
Except for Carol. She absolutely hated me and I had no idea
why.

Does she really hate you   I don't really think so

I was told that I started walking when I was eight months
old. That was really young
You were trying to run away   i just want to go back
I don't remember too much then until I was three. I guess I
needed my tonsils and adenoids taken out because I was
snoring so loud no one could sleep.
is that why everyone hates me   yes

I remember two events in the hospital when I went in for surgery. I remember the scary mask they put over my face and the really weird smell.   **youaredyingagaintommydying** Then I remember the day my mom got me dressed and I was sitting on the side of the bed waiting for the doctor to come in. It was Dr. Denton. I didn't remember him from before, but his grin looked evil and I was afraid. **helookedlikethedevil**   I remember mom started laughing, then got really mad when I was so scared. She grabbed me by the arm and we left.   **sheismadatyouagainlikeshealwaysis** why are you so mad at me momma   what did i do   you always make me feel really bad   and you're always mad   **hahahaha**

There would be times when my mom would absolutely just shut down. We have all experienced a "cold shoulder" but I don't think you've really experienced it unless you have met Betty. Absolute silence. And if looks could kill dad and I would have been dead way before I had a chance to live. Funny, it never seemed like I had a chance. When I would ask my dad what to do about mom, his stock answer was, "you know how she is, Tommy".

i'm sorry mama   i'm sorry   i know it is all my fault   it always is

There were usually two ways mom would warm up again. If I apologized. But for what? I never did anything that I could think of that I did wrong. Even my dad would tell me I didn't do anything. Mom held dad, me, and everyone else to

24

a very high standard. When the mood would lift and there would be a few days where it seemed like things were better, dad would often tease her and call her Mother Superior. She would laugh and laugh.

I am sure I am not exaggerating when I say this would happen four or five times a year, for as long as I can remember. I even remember many years later when I finally told my parents that I was getting a divorce. It was in January right after the holidays. Mom's reaction..."Why are you doing this to me? How can you do this to me? You're taking my granddaughter away from me. I'll never see her again. And it's all your fault". When I said to her "do you have any idea how I am feeling", she slammed the phone on me. That was January. I would call home every two weeks, dad would always answer the phone, which rarely happened in our house, but I knew she was listening on the other phone. He would often say she was out, and occasionally said she couldn't come to the phone right then. Remember, this was January. When I called on Mothers' Day, in May, she answered the phone and cried. Then she proceeded to tell me the story that she had been married before. She never once asked me how I was doing. Of course nothing ever changed as far as her seeing her granddaughter.

One time during one of her silent tantrums, I was about three years old, and I was in the kitchen asking her if I could go down the street and visit my friend, Martha, she wouldn't answer me. I started screaming and crying and I screamed "I hate you mom". She replied "I hate you too, Tommy". **andshedid**

i just don't know why you hate me momma   you always hate me momma
what did i do

You are so young, Tom, you wouldn't understand

The thing that was always so weird is that whenever we were around anyone outside of our immediate family, she would brag about how smart I was, what a good boy I was, and how her life wouldn't be the same without me. **lieslieslies** In fact, when we were doing anything outside of our home, mom would be fun, silly, and everyone loved her. I always loved when my cousins would come, especially the ones from Ohio. We would cook out, go to movies, play cards. But the other times it was really bad.

One day I came out of my room and mom asked me who I had been in there talking to. **uhoh** Carol was often very quiet, so she knew it wasn't her. I told her I was talking to my friend. She asked me what my friend's name was, and I said "Rankso". She   didn't   bat   an   eye. **butshehastothinkyouarecrzynow** She asked me where I met him, how I knew him, what we talked about, and I made up a very elaborate story about him. **allyoudoislie** I told her where he lived, where he went to school, that we talked about fun things, and he kept me company when I was alone. And that I loved him.   She still didn't bat an eye. **butshethoughtyouwerelying**   This was one of the first times I actually thought she listened to me, and that she liked me.

I know what she is like Tom   You don't have to talk about her   I want to know about you

This was the first time I felt heard. Understood. Liked. Maybe this is what love is.   Rankso and I would talk for hours. He would ask me questions, you know, good ones, fun ones.

nobody understands me like you do Rankso

Most of the time mom and Carol were fighting, yelling and screaming. Carol would run away. Mom would find her. I started developing the habit of holding my hands over my ears. I did it all the time. I would ask mom something and hold my hands over my ears when she answered, and then I would ask Carol what she said. Carol would look at me very oddly, but I did it, all the time. I was petrified that something would go wrong and she would get mad again.

When I was five I started kindergarten. I loved it. It got me out of the house and that energy. I remember the teacher was really nice. We would have playtime and learning time and nap time and snack time. There are two things that I distinctly remember like it was yesterday. One day a lady from the Louisville Orchestra, a flutist, came to give us a music lesson. Other than a guitar, I had never seen a real musical instrument up close. I remember going home really excited telling mom that this lady had this silver flute, and all of a sudden she made it get small and it played really high up. It was many years later when I realized it was a piccolo, and it was a separate instrument. I was mesmerized by the whole thing.

momma told me to calm down again   that's all she says to me when she's not mad at me   calm down tommy

The second strong memory was very different, and very confusing. We were having playtime, and the teacher had brought out a lot of clothes so we could play dress up. I grabbed a shiny black skirt. I put it on my head, put it on like it was supposed to go, and my teacher screamed at me that that wasn't for little boys to be playing with. **butthisiswhoyouaretommy**

something is wrong with me   i'm different from anyone else   i'm scared no one will ever like me   i don't know what it is   but it is bad   i'm only five but it is wrong   i'm really weird   **yesyouare**

Trust me Tom   you will be fine   It will take time

It was many years later when I realized I was gay. I think in junior high school I started to see it more, but I didn't understand it.

thoseboysnakedintheshowerroomaftergymclassyouloveditadm itit   I remember sneaking around the public library and trying to find anything I could about this, but remember when I was in seventh grade it was the early 1960's and nothing like this was ever talked about. Ever. And in my family, I figured it was never going to come out. How could it, when I thought my mom didn't like me anyway.

i promise to be good mamma i won't be bad anymore **dontfuckingbelieveit**

You are not bad Tom   you are not bad

   Then we would go through a bit of time that seemed easy. Mom and Carol would be getting along better. Mom and dad, too. Carol was six years older than me until she had her birthday in November, then she would be seven years older until I had my birthday in April. One day she came home from school and was very animated, which was not her usual mood. I was sitting on the green couch we had back then and mom was on the other end of the sofa, and Carol was standing in front of me talking about something I knew nothing about.

But you did Tom   you did

In her science class that day, the teacher started talking about astral projection.

i wonder what that is   **thisisacrockofshittom**

You already know what that is Tom

She was showing us an exercise that her teacher had shown them, which I do not remember since I felt like I was disappearing.

i feel like i am floating   but i can't tell mamma   she would be mad at me and send me to my room   the strangest thing was happening   i am sitting beside myself too   now i am really scared   i can't hear anything they are saying   i just keep seeing me sitting beside me

I was having an out of body experience, which I don't think I had ever had, but I do remember having dreams all the time like I was flying. Mom was very quiet and I was so surprised that she was so attentive. I don't ever recall her being so interested in what Carol had to say. They were fighting most of the time. All I remember is that I felt I had to never think about that anymore. It was the beginning of summer vacation after first grade and how was I to know about these things.

Tom you've already been doing this for a very long time You just didn't know what it was   But it is time you know about these things

I don't ever remember telling mom that story, even as an adult. As years went by I did learn a few interesting things about my mom that I am really grateful for. She did have some interesting "powers". **nofuckingwayshewajustabitch**

I remember one time at dinner, my mom asked dad about someone that he used to work with that they hadn't seen in a really long time. The phone rang. Dad rarely answered the phone, but for some reason he did get up from the dinner table and answered it. I remember him coming back to the table and he looked like the blood had drained right out of his face. All he said was "it's for you Betts". When mom went to the phone all I heard her say was "well we were just talking about you". That wasn't the first time something like that happened. In fact these things with mom happened very often. Many years later whenever I would bring up my 'interesting' thoughts my mom would always be really interested and would sit and listen for hours. I really appreciated those times with her because I didn't have many people I could talk to about those things.

i know something you don't know   i know something you don't know   i say it over and over in my head

Yes you do Tom   You know all   You have just forgotten for awhile

So the summer after I had that first revelation was a really pivotal summer for me. It was 1958 and I was six. My dad's sister and her family were living in the west end of Louisville right beside the house that dad grew up in. It wasn't the best of neighborhoods, but what does a six year old know of that, at least back then. I was dropped off there in the morning and mom and dad and Carol were all dressed up and went somewhere without me. I remember playing with my cousin and had a really fun time.

something weird is happening   i just know it   i don't know why but i just do

You know, only a few times did I ever think my mom actually did something deliberately. Her reactions, and actions, although quite unpredictable, were just that. Totally pre meditated and very deliberate.

are you mad mom

I used to ask my mom pretty relentlessly if she was mad. Not necessarily at me, just mad, perhaps at the world. But when you are four, five or six, that just isn't part of how you think yet. I know I was an emotional child but there are times when I just didn't feel that my mom recognized that.

What happened to Betty when she was two shaped the direction of her life It's not about you Tom   she had a life way before you came along and you need to remember that

As the years went on I am sure, no, I know I had hoped she would mellow. She did in certain ways. When she moved to Chicago in 1999 I think being close to me made a bit of a difference, but as time marched on I think I just became even more of the focus for her. One of my friends, a beautiful healer I knew, told me once how lucky I was that Carol was the focus in my early years. She made me wonder what my life might have been like if Carol hadn't been in the picture and all of the focus from mom would have been on me. It was already hard enough.

You know that wounding at age two is really interesting. Now that I have had the time, education, and life in years I now see how almost all of her relationships lasted about two years. How very curious. She would have just the dearest friend for about two years, then there would be something that the 'other' one might not do that my mom had really hoped for. My mom went out of her way to try and please people. Make dinner, make plans, go on outings, bought things. But she smothered everyone to the point that they just couldn't take it anymore. There would be one small thing that would trigger her and that would be it. Mom would literally throw a fit and all I would hear would be how she was ignored, how she was never invited to their home, how they never called. You name it, that's what would happen. Every time. The list of friendships, family members, ministers, neighbors, well the list could just go on and on. They never lasted, and she would grieve in her own way and move right along. Mom outlived all of her siblings, and if I remember she only had two, her brothers Ralph and Maurice were the only ones that she ever talked about affectionately. There was something about the others that she just couldn't bring herself to remain in contact with. But the two year limit really fascinated me until I understood more about woundings and the effects in early childhood. And she always seemed to forget that these things ever happened. She had a way of doing that. Making everything disappear like they never happened.

i always fear that she will make me disappear

Mom could actually be the life of the party. She loved to entertain, of course she loved being the center of attention. I had many colleagues who would often say how when they were her age that they hoped they would be just like Tom's mom.

but it doesn't matter mamma   i just wait for the next time   because there is always a next time

Betty worked and drove until she was ninety. Yes, she was one of those ladies that you find in CostCo or Sam's Club that would give you a sample of something to eat. Often she was the lead demo person of the month. I sometimes thought that she must have chased people down the aisle until they finally bought whatever she was sampling. But the truth is that she was really loved by everyone in the work environment. After ninety, she began to have more memory problems, some difficult behaviors and life began to be very challenging. My wonderful partner Nick was a Godsend to me. As much as I always hated her behavior, he would be there as a buffer for me, as a help. The more she became comfortable with Nick, the more she let her guard down and he saw the sides to her that I had always seen. And that made me feel validated. Someone really saw and understood what I had been going through my whole life.

Right after New Years 2013, in fact on January 3, mom hosted a big holiday party. Among several very close friends, my daughter and granddaughter were visiting. We had a really great time but I could see how my mom was really beginning to fade.

Our condos looked side by side from the outside, but they were actually one above the other. The lower one was moms and she had no steps inside of her place to deal with, and one bedroom and bath. The one upstairs was the largest of condos in the complex with three bedrooms and two bathrooms. When you came in from the garage you would find a closet and stairs. We cut through the closet and made a doorway that connected the units, but had a door for privacy. I felt I needed to be able to get to her on a moment's notice.

After the party we had gone upstairs for the evening and everyone had left. I heard a somewhat familiar but unsure voice yell up from the staircase, "Tom, what do I wear to work?" I knew something was wrong. When I went down to check on mom, she was really confused. I reassured her, found her work clothes in her dryer and went back upstairs, having more than my usual concerns. In the morning I went down early to check on her, since she was to report to work at 9 am. She said

"I don't think I should go to work today". I agreed and suggested she call her boss, which she did. And then she said, "I don't think I should drive anymore".

I only said okay. And that was the beginning of the end. Mom never went back to work and I am grateful that she never mentioned driving again. One of my big fears was that we would be battling over the car keys, but that didn't happen.

One thing led to the next, her dementia continued and one Thursday night in February, right before Valentines Day Nick called me while I was teaching and mom had fallen and he couldn't get her up off the floor. I raced home, got mom onto the bed. She was actually in a good mood. She didn't want me to call a doctor or an ambulance. I gave her two ibuprofen, helped her to go to the bathroom, then put her to bed. I thought we would be up in the night, and sure enough we heard banging downstairs about two am. She had fallen as soon as she got out of bed and was swinging the bathroom door and it was banging against the wall. I called the ambulance and got her to the hospital. Very shortly the doctor came in and told us what we had already figured, she had broken her hip. She went through the surgery well and then I was tasked with finding a rehab place for her to go to. There was a wonderful place very near home and that is where she was, continuing to decline, until Christmas Day

2014. Alden of Waterford. I would often arrive to see her and she thought I was her brother Ralph. She would ask how things were at home , but I knew she was referring to her childhood home in Ohio, because often she would ask why her mom didn't want her to come home anymore. It was heartbreaking, to say the least. Mom had been very 'with it' until about 91 years old, and then she went downhill fast. The last time I actually spoke with her was when I visited on that Christmas Day. Her last words to me were 'I love you'. The next morning I got a call that she had been taken to the hospital. She never spoke to me again. The doctor was wonderful and she was very direct but oh so kind when she gave me the list of hospices to be considered. How interesting that I had often driven from home to school and watched a building grow, and it ended up being the very hospice she went to. It was two minutes from home. Allegra and Satya arrived on New Year's Day, which was a Thursday. Allegra went with me to see her that day. I went and spent time with her on Friday, and when Nick and I were there on Saturday the 3rd we were there for about two hours hearing what is called the death rattle which was very present. All of a sudden there was a shift in her breathing, and about fifteen minutes later Nick said that he thought something was happening. The next bit of time seems on one hand like one minute, and at the same time it seems endless. I noticed the room was getting dark, and to me it had a distinct purple glow. Mom was looking directly at me and I felt her energy very strongly as though she was giving me a gift. Although I believe I was in a trance, I was very aware of what was going on and felt my whole body receiving that gift. After she took her final breath I felt her spirit go right through me. It took my breath away, but it was so beautiful. I went to find the nurse and of course she had passed. And it's just like everyone I know has said to me, even though it is totally expected, there is shock. The nurse asked me if we could leave the room for a short time while she prepared her. I made the necessary calls and we went back to the room until they arrived to take her away. I have to say the whole experience was not only amazing, but the kindness I felt from everyone was really touching and helped me a lot through the process. Of course Nick was with me the whole time, and we then went home. Allegra said she and Satya both had looked at the clock at exactly noon, and that is precisely the time she passed.

You fulfilled the promise Tom   You took care of her until she passed   The gift she gave you was incredible as you will find in the years to come

I am sure I lost count of the number of times I heard mom say in our years together "I'm snakebit". She thought being the seventh child was unlucky and that's why she felt she had bad luck her entire life.

Mildred Elizabeth "Betty" Wermuth

3/24/1922 - 1/3/2015

. . .

What an incredible life my mom lived. When I reflect back I see an early wounding, then as a teenager she lost her brother Dick to tuberculosis, was married and was deserted, married my dad and in her 20's then lost her favorite brother Ralph in a horrible accident, was told she would never bear children, and adopted a daughter that she thought hated her.These changes alone are enough to make her feel 'snakebit'. It makes parts of my life seem so easy by comparison. I have a few close friends who know what my mom could be like, and wonder how I could continue to love her and take care of her. But she was my mom and we had met at some point before in the Universe. I am very aware, most definitely between lifetimes, that we had made a pact. My part was that I would take care of her til the end of her time here in this lifetime. And she was absolutely my greatest teacher in this lifetime for me. That was what she promised me.

She had always expressed that she wanted to be beside my dad in Kentucky. I had her cremated immediately and on September 1st we drove to Louisville and placed her ashes beside my dad Lorney. Nick and one of my dearest childhood friends were there with me. I played a recording of

Massenet's 'Meditaion from "Thais"', my lovely friend sang 'Amazing Grace', and they gave me as much time as I felt I needed there with her by myself. She had always said that she wanted the Meditation to be played at her funeral. I was overwhelmed with grief.

The day before I had the good fortune to visit my old violin teacher Mrs. French, who was still teaching at the age of 86. She was very energetic and enthusiastic and it was as though the forty years since I had seen her last just melted away. I couldn't believe how much she remembered from my lessons, what I played, how I played, what I played for my audition at Juilliard. But the best part of the visit was right before we left. I would like to include the end of an article I wrote after:

When I ended my visit at the Louisville Music Academy, I took the opportunity to share some really personal feelings with Mrs. French in a private moment. I told her that I didn't have the easiest childhood growing up, but the one thing I completely took away from my lessons was her love. As each lesson ended, somehow, in words, or a gesture, even a smile, I left her school knowing that I was going to be just fine. It wasn't always about playing the violin. It was so much more than that. She just looked at me, gave me that smile like always, said she knew, and we said goodbye. I am so glad I got to have that moment with her. It made me realize that the hour or two we spend each week with our students may just be one of the best hours in their entire week. And that hour might just be one of the best for me, a teacher, too.

On the drive back to Chicago, the highway was closed for construction. There were no clues or detours, we just had to get off the highway. I wasn't at all sure where we were going, so I went in the direction I thought we should go. Suddenly I noticed a flock of birds flying over us, and they continued to fly with us for several miles. When I finally knew we had been going the right way, they were gone. My mom was clearly looking after me, and I felt a great sense of peace as we continued home.

There was also one other interesting event that I want to share. When I would leave for school there were a few ways I could go. Some days I would drive past the hospice she was in when she passed, other days I would go left instead of right and hop onto the expressway. All of a sudden on this particular day I went to the right, which was not the way I was planning to go, and after I turned I saw in my rearview mirror a semi-truck went right through the light and smashed into about five cars that were turning left. If I had gone the way I planned I would have been the first car to get hit. I drove past the hospice and waved. My heart felt so full.

Tom do you remember that as a child after the experience of Carols tale of astral projection that you would always sit by the living room window and watch for her to walk from the bus stop home You thought you were looking for her mood before getting home but the truth is you were seeing and reading her energy field a skill you continued to use at the music school by looking out the window there for people to arrive And you didn't even know it until your daughter asked you if you were aware that you spent time doing it every day It wasn't until you did your energy training that you were aware

Clearly she was the teacher you needed in this lifetime.

Orphaned

Carol was born on November 18, 1946. Her mom was Beth and her dad was Ralph Gordon, Betty's brother. She was the middle child, with an older brother Kenneth and a younger sister Susan. It was the summer of 1948 when Ralph was killed in the construction accident. I can only sit and ponder what that family, well in fact the whole Gordon family felt. But what I find really interesting is that her birth mother, Beth, really didn't want Carol. Kenneth and Susan were kept together, Carol was sent to live with my mom and dad. My mom was always willing to help her family out, sometimes perhaps a little too heavy handed, but I know Betty's intentions were in her heart. It seemed only when she was criticized that her temper flew into a rage when she felt unwanted or unneeded. She always felt like she was being used.

As I mentioned in the previous chapter, the early wounding of a two year old creates such an abandonment issue. How utterly fascinating that Carol was sent to mom.

No accident at all

When one is abandoned it seems that everything they need and do makes it all about them. They just can't afford to be left again, at any cost. The attention that they require just to be able to survive is monumental. I remember when I did my advanced training at the healing school we were in class one day and two of the students got into a bit of a heated argument about their friendship, and I had such a knee-jerk reaction. I immediately wanted to leave my body (which I was quite prone to do). One of the teachers looked at me and asked if I was okay. I suddenly flashed back to the arguments that mom and Carol would have, and how I never physically ran away because something in me would have to stay.

You were guardian of both your mom and Carol

Dear Carol,

I've wondered for fifty years where you went, what you did, who you were, and whether you are still here or not. **butremembershehatedyoutom** I only had a few friends that knew about you, and then even fewer that knew our story. I can't tell you the number of times I have been asked, why do you still care? Or even more, how could you still say you love her? But

Love never stops Tom, never ever

it is so interesting how certain things will always be burned into ones being for every lifetime. I remember that first time you tried to kill me. I thought you hated me. Little did I know. When you sneaked into the room, mom and dad's room where the crib was, I felt your hatred. I couldn't move,

44

and I don't even remember crying right away, until it happened.

what is that horribleness mamma where are you daddy where are you who is this

 i do not understand what is happening to my earthly body right now you decided that i needed to not be there so you could feel safe, so you pulled my head in between the crib bars and started twisting it

 is this what they call pain

I could hardly breathe. I remember screaming, and in fact I do not think I stopped crying for at least a year.

i don't know what is happening

Suddenly the door opened and this woman appeared
And I was right behind her
And I thought someone was behind her, but it wasn't daddy where are you daddy
The woman was our aunt who was married to my uncle Tom, dad's brother, whom I was named after.

lawrence thomas wermuth april third 1952 named after dad's brother tom 11:32 am saint anthony's hospital louisville kentucky lawrence was a long time family name daddy was lawrence john his dad was lawrence george and the farthest back i can remember is lawrence joseph lawrence thomas was the name i would carry around in this lifetime

Almost gone, hardly breathing, my aunt picked me up to comfort me, but it seemed hopeless. I remember daddy coming home and it was better

but where is mamma

Mom, I was told years later, started hemorrhaging and needed blood transfusions so was rushed back to the hospital.

i was left with my aunt and you   does mamma hate me   why did I do this to her   i don't understand   did you even know what you were doing   much less why

Carol had such hatred for her   She thought your mom took her from her own mother   why wouldn't she

I do not remember a lot of time after that, probably not until I was five and went to kindergarten. I think I began to wake up then. I remember Friday nights when we would make popcorn, maybe even grilled cheese sandwiches in that funny iron thing that you held on the stove burner and the sandwiches came out round. How I loved those nights. That's when I would catch myself covering my ears and asking mom if Carol and I could split a coke, and then have to look at Carol for the answer. I was always so afraid of mom rejecting me. It was awful. But then Carol would look at me and whisper she said yes. I loved those nights.

I also loved when mom and dad would leave you to look after me. Peculiar that I didn't ever feel unsafe with you at those times, no matter what you tried to do to me before. And I never expected you to do anything to me. You always had such strange things to tell me. Your stories were really fascinating and I often wondered if you were from a different planet. I remember that time you introduced me to a seance and we had a lit candle. I don't remember what must have startled us, but you tried to hide the candle under your bed. Then all of a sudden the bed was on fire. I remember running to the refrigerator and getting that glass bottle mom kept in there for cold drinking water. It couldn't have held more than about three cups, but there I was throwing it on the underside of the bed. I think you ran across the street and got Faye Underwood and you both came running across the street. I don't remember too much more because I was gripped in fear for mom to come home.

All I remember from then on were the horrible arguments between you and mom, and I remember dad talking less and less and was really sad.

What about the diary, Tom   The one your mom found

Then there was that day when mom and dad took you to see a doctor. I was at our aunt's house and only remember a bit.

what happened   what happened   what is this diary she found

And the two other times she tried to kill you Tom

47

There was that time when we were at the swimming pool and you were supposed to be looking after me, but you teased me badly about being a baby and a chicken. You were in the deep end of the pool and you taunted me to jump in, so I did, and you climbed out and laughed at me until the lifeguard had to jump in and get me. I remember walking away from you thinking I would never let anyone do that to me again. Ever.

You also hated me playing the violin. It was one of the things that mom seemed proud of me doing. You used to make me practice in the garage in the middle of winter after school. You and one of your boyfriends tried to kill me again. He held me on the garage floor while you tried to pour Clorox down my throat, but I got away. Oh my, I don't believe that I remember these things like they were yesterday.

And that was the last time

I remember one of the worst times between you and mom. Mom had come home early from work one day and I was just home for school. Something was really off that day. I thought something must have happened to dad, or you. Then all of a sudden there was a noise in the kitchen and there you were trying to climb in that really small kitchen window. For some reason mom had locked the door when she came in and you couldn't get in the door. Apparently mom had gotten a call from your school. You had an after school job working in the high school main office. With all the screaming that was going on I figured out that you had somehow gotten to where they stored report cards, and you had made a duplicate with good grades and brought it home for mom and dad to see, then forged their signature and took it back. I just remember you storming off to your room and mom once again was silent for at least a week, making everyone feel as though we all had done something very wrong.

you are always so unfair mama

On November 18th, 1964 you left. I woke up early hearing mom crying in the living room, and you had packed a bag and left. It was your 18th birthday. There was a small amount of inheritance from a trust fund from your birth father, Ralph. I don't know how much I just remember that you got something when you turned eighteen. I went to the living room to comfort mom but she was inconsolable. It was so very sad.

For a few years mom and dad tried to keep the family together. You married a guy named Bobby and had two kids, Kenneth (named after your birth brother) and Victoria. I remember visiting one time and you got really angry at Victoria's crying and crying, and she was lying face down on the sofa, she was probably three or four months old, and you swatted her so hard she flew into the air. I remember you looking at me and laughing as though you didn't mean it, but it was one of the times I was actually really scared of you.

Sometime after that I remember mom getting a phone call from a private detective. You were missing. No one knew where you were or what happened. Bobby was heartbroken and you had deserted your two kids. Victoria was only two.

In May of 1969, the year before I was graduating from high school, there was a knock early one evening and there you were at the door. Mom let you in, and you told us you had married someone else and you were living in Nashville Tennessee. You had a little boy with you, his name was Bryon. You asked me if I would come visit sometime and I had such mixed feelings about it, but my instinct told me to say probably not just because mom was there and I thought she would be mad. You left shortly after that and I remember when the door shut mom said she looked in your eyes and knew you were pregnant again.

The Christmas of my senior year I took a bus to see you. I remember your husband, Byron (that is where the name Bryon came from) drove a VW bug and drove only in first and second gear and it was so fast I was petrified. We pulled up to what seemed to be a deserted house in the middle of nowhere and you lived in an apartment on the second floor. When I got up there you were there with the little boy and a fairly newborn girl. I don't recall what her name was. I wasn't able to sleep all night, and in the morning I remember calling home and I didn't want to stay. I didn't feel comfortable. For the first time in my life I actually was afraid of you, and Byron. You put me on a bus in the afternoon and I was home by the evening.

And she disappeared   again

Shortly after that we got a call from someone, I don't know who, that you had disappeared again. Once again you left a little boy and a girl, who was about two.

I went away for part of the summer and when I came home all pictures and any reminders of you had disappeared from our house. It was so very strange. It was as though you had never existed, and for many years not one word was ever spoken about you never it was as though you had died and mom always introduced me as her only child it was so very strange for me and I hated lying

A few years later mom gave me a letter that had come for me, from you. You had changed your name to Suzanne Elizabeth Gordon and you were living in Arizona. Suzanne was the name mom would have given me if I had been a girl. Elizabeth was mom's middle name. Gordon was your birth name, and mom's maiden name. Arizona was where mom sister Jeannie lived. And the only other thing was that you were planning to get married once again and move to California.

and that was the last time i ever heard from you   i haven't seen you since December of 1969   that is almost 53 years   i tried to find you a number of times throughout the years   but never did

Carol kept recreating her own childhood. She was abandoned by her own mother, hated and blamed Betty, and two times that you know she left her own children. Always when the youngest was two.   What a very strange thing to do.

and you left me

Carol, I still wonder to this day whatever happened to you. Truthfully I don't know whether you are still alive or dead. My gut tells me you are no longer in this lifetime. I just wish I knew and had closure.
And you finally figured out that in all those pictures where you thought the hatred was directed at you, it was actually your mom she truly hated. You thought Betty had taken you away from your own mom, but the truth is that Beth gave you up on her own.

Love, Tom

Carol Lee Wermuth
11/18/1946 - unknown

I Died

And then that fateful day when so much happened   It was a scorching July day in Kentucky and you were at your aunts house playing with your cousin and his friends in their front yard   They lived right next door to where your dad was born   Your aunt was on the porch chatting well more like gossiping with a friend   Everyone thought you had a really bad summer cold because your sinuses were so stopped up   but I know differently

You always loved playing with both your Ohio and Kentucky cousins   You didn't have many friends and usually the only ones you talked to were your mom and dad and Carol and of course me   So playing with different kids you knew was a real treat for you

While you were playing you started sneezing...and sneezing...and sneezing and the amount of mucous coming out of you was not only huge but at a frightening pace   You kept choking and coughing and sneezing Your aunt came running with some paper towel or something like it   but it was useless   Whomever she had been talking to one the

porch came running out with a hand towel which was
better   You were absolutely scared frozen

i remember thinking that i was going to die   but then that feeling went away
quickly and i thought   i am losing my best friend   what am i going to do

You will be fine Tommy   Always remember I am with you
Your constant companion   And you will always be able to
talk to me if and when you need to   You may not see me for
awhile but I promise I am there

Your body finally collapsed on the lawn but I told you you
would be fine   After lying still for what seemed like forever
you got up   It all had happened so fast   The kids were
laughing at the snot that came flying out of you while your
aunt and that lady are more concerned that you were okay
You were   They all noticed once the energy settled down
that not only were you fine you had no signs nor sounds of
having any kind of cold or sickness   Do you remember
This will revisit you in years to come   Right now it almost
seems like a dream

i didn't feel sick anyway   i never did   i felt as though something or someone
was inside me trying to come out   it was really scary   but something kept
telling me i was okay   so i knew i was   i am sure it is Rankso holding me

Your energy field was brilliantly shining and you were ready for what would come next   The next thing was that lady asking your aunt where your mom and dad were   You overheard her saying that they had to take Carol to see a doctor   you know   the kind that we don't ever talk about She whispered psychiatrist

i don't know what that is i hate doctors they scare me i bet Carol is scared and mad but they wouldn't let me go with them mom just said it didn't concern me dad seemed really scared and sad i wished i was with them and not here

And then with perfect timing the car pulled up on the street in front of the house   Mom and dad got out and mom made Carol get out too   Carol looked really sad   and mad   and refused to say 'hi'   That made your mom really mad and Carol got back in the car and slammed the door   Mom said everything was fine when my aunt asked her but you knew she was lying   Everyone was trying to tell your mom what had just happened to you   but she didn't want to listen and she grabbed you by the hand and you and your dad and mom got in the car

daddy was driving and mom was in the other front seat i was behind mom and Carol was behind dad nobody talked Carol just looked so sad and kept staring out the window the silence hurt

The trip back home usually took about 40 minutes   We lived in the south end of Louisville and there were no highways back then   It was the summer of 1958 and so very very hot

i am really nervous my stomach hurts i'm scared what's going to happen i hope i didn't do anything wrong mom will be so mad when we get home i hate this it's taking forever to get home **feelingguiltyareyou**

It seemed like an eternity to you   The silence must have lasted at least half an hour   Your dad turned onto Eastern Parkway and you knew you were getting close to home

Tommy, you never talk about Rankso any more. Whatever happened to him?
You were frozen.
i don't know how to answer
Be careful Tommy   how you answer is really important   I can help

where did you go Rankso i'm scared i don't know what to say i feel so tired i want to sleep and not be here

You probably don't remember what I told you but suddenly you said
mamma Rankso died   he was at that place on Feastern Parkway just up here on the right

You were right now passing a funeral home you had seen many times on the trip home

What happened Tommy? Did he really die? How?

yes mamma   he really did   i never see him anymore   he died and i just never

see   him   anymore   one   day   he   just   disappeared

andyouknewthiswholetimeyouwerelying

Are you sure Tommy? You never see him any more?

i don't   he's gone

And just like that I died   You thought you never heard from me anymore for a very long time   But I am always here for you   you just have to ask

But you don't know why it seemed like I went away

I am going to tell you now but you won't understand nor remember for many years to come

maybe i should have just told her the truth   you are still here   still my best

friend in the whole world   why would you leave me   i thought there was an

unspoken promise

So once day you will remember   You will understand why just today   now   why she was asking you about me Doesn't it seem too oddly coincidental that your mom and dad took Carol to see that doctor today and then a short time later she asks about me   Don't you see that she was testing you   Your mom always thought that the problems with Carol were her fault but she never spoke it   What if

57

you turn out the same   What if you became angry and lied all the time   She still accuses you of lying enough and you know that you don't   The only time you have held back the truth is to protect either yourself or Carol   You have been Carols protector all along   What if she thinks you are turning out just like Carol   That would totally end her world   So she had to know if you still had and imaginary friend   And if you did that would mean she was right   that you would turn out to be just as much trouble as Carol   Carol was bad   every day   She lied and cheated all the time   Maybe she asked the doctor about you too   After all she thought it was not normal to have an imaginary friend   Maybe there is something wrong with you and it will just be a matter of time until you start lying and cheating and what if its actually all Bettys fault

But there was something else Tommy   You knew that Carol had a diary she kept locked   didn't you   Your mom was always looking in her belongings for something   a clue   a hint and answer for why she behaved the way she did   So she found the diary and got it open

It was when she read the diary that Carol had said that she was going to try and kill you   Maybe try more than once   We know she did when you were a bit older   twice   Once at then pool and once in the garage with her friend

You are her golden boy Tommy   She loves you so very much
she just has a tough time showing anyone   She just can't get
past herself   And there will be many times she will tell you
that she loves you when you get older but you won't always
believe it   because she won't always be able to show you
Because of her own wounding when she was two and her
many losses she won't be able to get past them all   And she
will believe it has all been her fault   That is a tough load to
bear though one's lifetime

You will remember all of this one day   but for now you must
travel through the sea of forgetfulness for awhile   I know it
will go by in a flash   but you won't   It will   seem like it takes
a very long time

So put me to sleep for now Tommy
I will always be here for you   but for now you must forget
Forget me
Today is the day I died
I love you Tommy

i will always love you Rankso   forever

Rankso
Unknown - July 1958

Grandma's Attic

I have a really lovely marble top table that I inherited from mom who inherited it from my grandma. It's the only thing mom wanted. My guesses are that Ida and Harry got married very young, before 1900, and I know this was a wedding present. I treasure it and so did mom. I know they got married young because mom told me the story of their engagement happening at a local fair, and grandma was only 16. I also inherited a beautiful tintype photograph that my mom had redone in color many years ago, and it's them in the park with a balloon. Another one of my treasures.

As you know they had eight kids, and I know they took a nephew in and for years I thought he was the youngest of the children, but I found out he was the son of my uncle Ed and his first wife. He was Harry and I loved him a lot and he was very fond of mom and came to visit often in Kentucky. I am not sure whatever happened to him.

Grandma was, now that I think carefully about it, really tired. She took care of a three story house in Middletown Ohio, and my grandad was a Methodist minister. That was before I was born. Rumor has it that he was dismissed as a minister for some mysterious reason, and if mom knew why she never shared it. I seem to remember she would get really silent when I asked, so I stopped asking many years ago. I think she really loved her dad a lot.

We used to go to visit every six weeks when dad had his long weekend from the milk routes. Back in the 1950's people dressed up when they traveled. Dad wore a suit and tie, had a really beautiful hat, and mom was also dressed to the nines. Dad smoked cigars back then so when we would go in the colder weather I hated it because the windows were always rolled up. Carol used to get carsick all the time so mom often brought flowers from her garden that had a really nice scent for us in case she did get sick in the car. Unfortunately we had to keep it under our noses often. Boy did I hate that! The ride took over three hours in the old days before the bigger highways were built. But I always looked forward to going. The house on Sutphin Street was big and scary and had so many really cool things in it.

The downstairs was a large living room that you entered from the entranceway. I remember loving the pocket doors that you opened to go in, sliding them in and out. The room was filled with every antique you could imagine, including the very table I now have, because grandma furnished the entire house by going to flea markets and rummage sales. Gosh do I wish I could go in there again now. There were

61

probably many valuable antiques that were hardly worth anything back then. The couch was a deep purple type of velvet that if you rubbed it one way it looked lighter in color. Everything was so mysterious. The room off of that was originally a dining room, but was now my grandparents bedroom as the other floors were needed for all the kids, and they never changed it back as they got older so they didn't have to climb the stairs every day. Then there was a bathroom and down that hallway came the huge kitchen where they had a rather large table where the family always ate. That was the usual place, to sit around their table and visit.

I loved the front porch and the backyard so much. The porch was filled with wicker furniture, a rocking chair that I thought was huge, but probably wasn't as big as I remember. The ashtrays were made from red clay they had found on vacation one year. I remember having to sleep out on the porch one time when the entire Gordon clan came for my grandparent's fiftieth wedding anniversary. We picked cherries from the big cherry tree in the back for grandma to make pies and my dad and grandad and I went in the 'machine' to the local Piggly Wiggly for food for the cookout. Between the adults and kids there must have been forty or so people. It was the only time I got to meet my cousins that were there from Arizona. I just remember having the best time.

The second floor had two bedrooms, a bathroom, and a small apartment with a living room, bedroom, bathroom and small kitchenette. That is where my grandma would rent out to single widowed women for a little extra money. I think back then they paid around ten dollars a month to live there. Then there was the very scary small staircase to the attic, which had been renovated for the girls in the family. How many stories I heard from mom where she and my aunt Helen had to share a bed. By the time I came along there were three large beds to sleep in, one just out in the big room, then there were two alcoves, one where Carol slept and on where mom and dad slept with a folding screen to give them some privacy. I remember being so afraid to go up there by myself. Carol would gladly go up, but I would try to stay awake and be in the kitchen where everyone was talking or snacking, or I would finally go into the living room.

nosylittlebrathadtoknoweverything

At some point dad would usually come and get me and take me upstairs. I don't ever remember going up there all by myself, even if Carol was there. I can still remember the smell of the old quilts my grandmother made, and the braided rugs I used to watch her make. I loved it. It was like being in a strange but fascinating mystery story.

But something kept calling me up there, so one day I braved it and......

i don't care if its scary   i have to go up there   i have to see what is up there......went up. *Look at those strange looking small closets over by where mom and dad sleep. Do you see them, to the right in the wall. Open the door* up

becarefultommytheremightbemonstersinthem

what in the world is this it looks like some kind of case   and there is something inside   kind like a small weird guitar

So open it up and look at it

I ran back downstairs and found mom and made her come up there with me. She told me it is a violin.

A violin   my my my

i don't know what a violin is mama

Then mom began telling me the story that her mom and dad made each of the eight kids take at least one year on a musical instrument. But that's all they got to do because moore lessons cost too much. Only aunt Helen was allowed to take piano lessons, that's why she plays well, and she was really the only one who took an interest in music at all. I loved that huge piano downstairs in the living room. I know I drove everyone crazy with my banging on the keyboard, but I would get music out of the bench and pretend I was playing it. It was pretty dramatic.

can we take it home can we please can we

Tommy I promised I will always be right by your side. All the time.

Mom right away said yes! I couldn't believe my ears. She said we could take it home and get it fixed up.

i can't wait

Patience Tommy Patience   this will last a lifetime

And it has been the love of my life. We took it back to Kentucky, took it downtown to a local music store called Durloffs and in a few weeks got it back.

A few months later we went back to visit and the strangest thing happened with my grandma. We had an adorable dachshund named Dutchess. Of course she went everywhere with us, and always loved grandma and would spend hours sitting in her favorite chair with her. Well, this time when we went Dutchess would have nothing to do with her. Wouldn't go near her and wouldn't even look at her when she called her. We all thought it was really strange. So, after we went back home and did the holidays that year and shortly after the new year we got a call. Grandma had cancer. Colon cancer. Mom was devastated.

Shortly after we got that call we were summoned back to Ohio for a family powwow. Aunt Helen flew in from California, Jeannie from Phoenix, Ed and Harry were local and uncle Maurice drove in from Illinois. I don't remember Bob being there. Everyone was gathered around the kitchen table with grandma and grandad. Nosy little me had to keep going in there in hopes of finding out something, so this one time mom took me into the living room and scolded me. Well of course I had to follow her right back into the kitchen, and the second the door opened my grandma was saying

"I can't go live with Betty. Tommy drives me crazy".

Of course mom went into a rage and ran out of there up the stairs to the third floor all the time holding my hand. When we got up there she started sobbing and I told her it was okay. But what transpired was pretty typical of my mom. It wasn't about me, it had to be about her. And, as usual, I ended up comforting her which is what always happened. It wasn't too long before we were in the car on our way back home. And it had been decided that grandma would just remain at home for the time being.

Later into the winter my grandma got much worse and I remember my mom would work Monday through Friday and leave after work to drive to Ohio and come back on Sunday night. No matter what, mom loved her mother very much. She was hospitalized and one Saturday night my best friend Charlie was sleeping over at my house and the strangest thing happened. I think it might have been around ten at night and I woke up startled and there was a white figure at the foot of my bed. It was my grandma, looking ever so beautiful and young again, like she looked in that old tintype

I have, and she told me she was sorry that she had said what she said. Just then the phone rang and my friend Charlie asked me who I was talking to, and all I said was that my dad was on the phone and I thought my grandma had died. That's all I said.

Be at peace again, Tommy

Sure enough my dad came in to tell me she had passed. I felt such a sense of love and peacefulness, I will never forget this visit. I never really thought that she hated me at all, for, I was a really hyperactive kid, but I can leave that for a bit later.

There was such a ruckus at the Gordon house in Ohio the weekend of the funeral. Apparently my grandfather had been having an affair. He had started the Golden Age Club in Middletown years before and at one point my grandma stopped going but we never knew why. Well I gather the affair had escalated quite a bit and the woman had moved into the house on Sutphin Street while grandma was in the hospital. Naturally my mom took offense to this, so we stayed in a motel in town and left right away after the funeral, once mom had collected the marble top table that she loved and wanted. Her mom had promised it to her and I know there was even an argument about that between the remaining siblings but Betty won out and it travelled back to Kentucky with us, and I am very happy to have it in my possession now, someday to be passed on to my daughter and granddaughter.

My grandad passed several years later, in his eighties, from a stroke. He and mom didn't speak again for all those years, and she went to see him when she heard he was in the hospital and as far as she told me they mended things between them. For awhile mom still seemed really mad at him, but as the years went on that seemed to fade and she would talk more affectionately about him.

Grandma was usually very quiet but sweet for the most part. Grandad scared me. He seemed very judgmental to me and that used to hit me a little too much for my comfort zone. But I did love going to visit because mom and dad really loved going there and I had some dear cousins I loved spending time with.

Ida Gordon passed at the age of 63 from colon cancer.
Harry Greenfield Gordon lived to be 83 and passed from a stroke.
I never knew the year they were each born.

little tommy tucker from tuckersville

*The first five
years have so
much to do with
how the next 80
turn out.*

Bill Gates Sr.

Definition of *coincidence*

1. the act or condition of <u>coinciding</u> **:** <u>CORRESPONDENCE</u>
... a perfect *coincidence* between truth and goodness ...
— Robert South

2. the occurrence of events that happen at the same time by accident but seem to have some connection
... causal connection requires something more than mere *coincidence* as to time and place ...
— Wayne R. LaFav

i was born on Thursday April 3rd 1952   interestingly i was due on March 24th which was my mom's birthdate but for some mysterious reason i was dragging my heels and it wasn't my time just yet   i believe that everything happens at the perfect time   for me what seems like a coincidence is merely just a 'hello' from the Universe to pay attention to whatever is going on right then

some people might even call it a wakeup call

Traditional Meaning of 'Far to Go'

Both positive and negative connotations have been associated with Thursday's child over the centuries. The traditional meaning is associated with Thursday children having a long, successful life without limitations. Going far in life is typically viewed as a positive attribute with children having a lot of potential and talent.

if you have read 'Sacred Contracts' by Caroline Myss then you might understand where i am coming from   it is no coincidence that i was "given" my parents   actually i believe it was my choice   everything we do we are both the teacher and the student   and sometimes what we need most to learn is through our teaching   and vise versa   i believe we all choose the people we encounter on our life train as well as the situations that occur   and it is all based on the lessons we need to learn   we revisit those lessons over over over and over   until we think we've gotten it   and just when we get to that point

we go to a deeper level   so many people look at this as a failure   i look at this
so positively because to me it means i am healing and growing   and that makes
me very happy and content to move on   as i have 'far to go'

i was six years old going into first grade in 1958   Mrs. White was my teacher
and of course when you are only six she seemed like she had to be at least a
hundred years old   the truth is she was most likely in her 40's and had been a
first grade teacher at Hazelwood Elementary for many years already   during
that first or second week we had a special visitor come into our class   his name
was Rubin Sher   and   oh how coincidental   he was trying to get new students
for his music class that met twice a week   it was a violin class   he was looking
for kids that might be interested in learning the violin   i immediately raised
my hand and said my mom had just gotten one fixed up for me and it was
sitting at home   Mrs. White told me to settle down as i tended to be really over
active   all the time   but Mr. Sher said for me to bring it to school   told me
what day and told my teacher to talk to my mom and dad   i am not sure exactly
what happened but the next thing i knew i was in the music room with several
other students   from that moment on time seemed to either pass really fast
or stand completely still   i do not remember another thing about first grade
except for violin class   there were three rows of students each sitting with a
music stand   on the stand was a pink grey and white booklet of music called
the Merle J Issac violin method   the man on the cover in the oval picture frame
also looked to be at least a hundred years old   with wire rimmed glasses
actually he kind looked much like my moms dad especially with the glasses
each row had a name   the first row was called the blockhead row   the second
was the okay row   and the third was the genius row   there were probably ten

or so students in the front row and less as we went back to the back row   the kids in the back row looked great with their violins and never got yelled at   it didn't matter to me if i got yelled at because i was actually learning how to play the violin   it was like a dream

one of my favorite memories is one time i was running to the bus stop after school   mamma got the bus home at 5 o'clock every day and the stop she got off was about three blocks away right in from of the ashland cleaners   i don't think i could stand still for one minute until she got off that bus and i yelled that i had made it to the genius row   already   now it was a dream come true   i think mom was happy for me but i honestly don't remember   and it actually doesn't matter   i was learning the violin for me

Exactly Tommy   and always remember that I AM the violin

it must have been shortly after that when we had our first night time assembly and the violin group played for all the parents and students that had come   after the concert my parents met Mr. Sher and he told then they should try and consider getting me private lessons   they asked him if he could give me the lessons but he didn't have any openings but knew of a teacher at a downtown music store   and soon i remember i was getting lessons from Miss Stoll   Miss Fanny Elizabeth Stoll   all i remember is she gave me weird flute music that had was too many flats   and in high positions other than first which she yelled at me for not knowing   she taught at Shackleton's Music Store downtown Louisville on fourth avenue in a really small studio in the basement and she would pace around me in circles and if she wanted me to play faster she would walk faster   she was over the top with hyper energy and my mom always said it took me the drive home and at least an hour to calm down after every lesson

it was also around this time that my mom had to take me to the doctor for some reason and he gave me these green and yellow capsules that i was to take morning noon and night   and they were called librium   i had no idea what it was   i would take one at breakfast and put one in my pocket to take at school lunch and one after dinner   by this time i was seven and in Mrs. Bard's second grade class   somehow i remember her talking at a parent meeting with my mom and i heard the word tranquilizer but didn't know what that meant

Don't worry Tommy   I will guide you

i remember the bullying at school   now it was the violin   on the days we had class we had to wait between the outside door and the door into the main hallways at the top of the stairs   boys would laugh at me   call me the sissy with the violin   and that i was a stupid girl   so i asked my mom if i could have a pillowcase to make a halloween costume which was a lie   and i started putting my violin in the pillowcase so no one would know what it was   and maybe it sort of worked   i still remember getting bullied anyway

maybeyouwereagirlyanddeserveditlittletommy

i also remember one day when i was walking to school i had an urge to throw the pill i had in my pocket on the ground   it was as though a voice inside my head was telling me to do it

Maybe

so i did   pretty much every day mom would ask me at the dinner table if i took my pill at lunch and i just lied   after about a month the tone of her voice began to change when she would ask me if i had taken my noontime dose   so i asked her if i seemed like i was being bad again   i have no idea why i said that i just did   she said no that she just wanted to know   i began faking that i was taking the morning pill and then i did it with the nighttime pill too   after some time she asked me again if i was still taking my noontime pill and that voice came back to me and said

If you are going to get by with this you are going to have to change your behavior

so i became very aware of when i would get really fast and hyper and tried my best to calm down   so the next time she asked i didn't lie and told her that i had not been taking them and all of a sudden she grabbed the bottle of pills and my hand took me into the bathroom and flushed the pills down the toilet and yelled that her child was not going to have to take these
i was shocked that she wasn't mad at me   she was just mad

   at some point mom got mad at Miss Stoll because she yelled at me during a recital that i had done the bowing the wrong way and before you knew it i was taking my private lessons with Mr. Sher   funny thing is the piece i had done the wrong bowing in i ended up in the future teaching for forty some years in the Suzuki Method   it is the first concerto in Suzuki book four by Frederick Seitz   and i must have taught it thousands of times in my career   and i loved it so much   coincidence   hmm

74

Mr. Sher was a wonderful teacher and mentor   i attribute my strong pulse and rhythmical sense to him   my lessons were either me standing or more often sitting with him right behind me   he smoked cigarettes like a fiend and often mom would say that i reeked of smoke when i came out of the lessons but more importantly he tapped the back of the chair one hundred percent of the time in my lessons with a pencil   not only could i hear it but i felt it constantly and for me that was the secret to an excellent sense of pulse   i have used tapping of a students shoulder or middle of the back and it is amazing how it help with internalizing the beat or pulse   but besides that Mr. Sher was a lovely man that i will always be grateful for him being one of my teachers

then came the summer after elementary school and i was preparing to go to Southern Junior High School which was about two blocks from my house   i was so excited about going to the new school and would be there through the ninth grade before moving on to high school   but that November was when Carol left home and things were not going so well at school   oh i did really well in my subjects but i was now getting bullied by older and bigger kids which hurt a lot more   and it seemed like i was confused all the time about me **andwhataboutyoursexualfeelingswhatareyougoingtodoaboutthat**

i went to an outdoor weekend in the fall where they had a bonfire when it got dark   apparently they had pulled a lot of poison ivy off of the logs and sticks they used for the fire and unbeknownst to everyone the poison can travel through smoke and when i went home i knew something was wrong   i had never had poison ivy or anything like it before and it was everywhere   on my eyelids in my nose   in my mouth   in my ears   all over my face and scalp and neck and hands   anywhere that was not covered by clothes that evening in fact is was so bad it looked like I had been burned in a really bad fire   it happened on a weekend so I didn't go to school for a week   we didn't have air conditioning then but dad ran out and bought a window air conditioner and put it in the living room window and i used to stand there all day long   by the next weekend i was feeling better so i went to school the next week even though i still looked like a monster   but i thought my friends would understand   i think i freaked the school nurse though because she wanted to send me back home but i convinced her that i was fine and she let me stay in school   i also think she must have called my mom at work too

   that was all fine until later in the week when i had to leave early for another doctors visit so he could give me an injection of cortisone because that seemed to be the only thing that could help   of course mom made me put on calamine lotion and that made me look even weirder   so when i was leaving the school to walk home which only took about three minutes wouldn't you know the worst bully in the school was outside by the back door smoking a cigarette   i think I remember his name was Jack but i am not sure   he started laughing at me and while i am not at all comfortable in this setting repeating exactly what he said he called me a faggot and asked me what was the gooey shit all over my face was   how did it get there   and it had to have been another guy who did it to me   i was so mortified   couldn't even speak much less defend myself so i just walked on home fast

hahahahaha

Confession

little did he know that in gym class in seventh grade all of the boys had to shower in the big shower room together then stand there waiting until the coach let us out to get dressed and i was beginning to have some really confusing thoughts about the other boys seeing them naked for the first time in my life my first real awakening about who i might really be and i hated it i was really afraid of my thoughts and feelings and had absolutely no one i could possibly talk to about it and i hated myself

it's no surprise to me now that shortly after Christmas i decided i wanted to quit the violin thinking maybe that is what was making me have those thoughts i just didn't know nor understand so i used the excuse that i didn't like that i had to come home and practice after school while all of my friends were bugging me about being outside and hanging out of course the other boys started calling me names too so i though if i quit that stupid violin that everything would then be fine

But of course that wasn't the case   you loved the violin and didn't want to quit   really

i didn't completely quit because i was taking orchestra for credit in school and i was in the Louisville Youth Orchestra which i loved so when about four months passed i asked my mom if i could start taking lessons again the truth is i missed it terribly practicing and lessons she actually said yes with one word of warning   if i ever decided to quit again that would be the last time i said that was fine when mom called Mr. Sher about me starting again he said he thought maybe it was time for me to have a different teacher so he recommended Ruth French i knew she was a very popular teacher and many of the really good violinists in the youth orchestra studied with her so mom called and i started with her in the summer she had eighty students and played full time in the Louisville Orchestra first violin section so the only time she had available right then was at 10am on Sunday mornings my dad bless him went to mass at 8 am so he would be home in time to drive me in for my lessons

And this was another angel sent to you on earth to help save your life Tom Ruth French an amazing being

lessons with Mrs. French were incredible i learned so many things in that first lesson and she gave me the most wonderful pieces to study i went home and think i must have practiced for four hours and the time flew by

Timing îs everything Clearly it was the right time for this new change But be careful Tom keep remembering what things can be like at home

no one had actually talked to me about vibrato i taught myself i remember when i first got into the youth orchestra the girl sitting next to me kept wiggling her arm and hand and it made the prettiest sound and i just kept watching listening and trying and before i knew it i could do it well at least that is what i thought and Mr. Sher just kept praising me about it so i thought it was good plus it sounded so grown up and i remember Mrs. French never said it was bad she just gave me new exercises to do to improve it

*Pay attention to her style of teaching Tom   It will mean
something in time to come*

   i almost felt like i was a beginner again given how much i looked forward to
every lesson   and she was so incredibly kind which wasn't necessarily what i
was used to   but she was completely direct and was never the type to beat
around the bush if she had to make a correction in my playing   this was just
the greatest thing that could have happened to me

and then there was the end of the summer right before eighth grade there was
a very small neighborhood grocery store that was about six blocks away
we only went there in the case of needing something right away and i never
remembered mom going in there she usually just sent me i think she thought
it was beneath her or something but there was this one day when she needed
to go so i thought i would go with her because the lady who worked at the
checkout was always so nice to me i could tell mom was in a bad mood i am
not sure if it was because she had to go in or something else   but she always
had this gray cloud around her when her mood was changing   so we got in
the car and went to the store

   when we got in the checkout line after shopping the lady was so nice to me
like she always was so i decided to put the groceries in the bags for her and just
as we were about to collect them and leave she said to my mom   "isn't it nice
to have such a strong young man helping you?"   and my mom immediately
replied   "him? Look at him. He's a weakling"   and the only way i can describe

how felt was that I had died right then to be honest i don't really remember
much of the ride home but i do remember that no one said a thing

Pay attention right now Tommy   or is it Tom now

I just had the most extraordinary memory while I am writing
this. I don't remember eighth grade. I don't remember
anything at all. I am seventy years old now and this is the
first time since that year that I actually realized I don't
remember a thing. It's like it didn't exist. I was just sitting
here and for some reason

Hmm

I was trying to remember who was my eighth grade math
teacher. For many years some of my teenage students would
ask me what my high school experience was like and I
remember someone asking me what year I took algebra and
I always said eighth grade. So just and hour or so ago I
started thinking about it and I thought, well I took algebra in
eighth grade, geometry in ninth, algebra two and trig in tenth
and   wait a minute that's not right because you then took a
semester of stats and a semester of probability in your senior
year but that's not adding up right. What the heck? Then I
tried to remember other things about eighth grade and I
couldn't remember any teacher, or my homeroom teacher or
even my orchestra director and that would have been
something I would totally remember. Well that year didn't
exist. In fact the next few years, although some things about

school pop up to me, it was like I was either sleeping, or when I do remember something, I feel like it was a dream. I remember being in a new school, now Iroquois High School, I loved orchestra, math and sciences. Also German class. It was so neat beginning to learn a new language and with a really amazing teacher that had a big influence on my own teaching in later years. I remember totally hating gym class, because of the one large shower room. I actually remember hiding in my locker until everyone was back out getting dressed. It was just horrible for me. I had a few teachers that I thought were just totally awesome. And now it seems like I was just starting to wake up.

As far as my sexuality goes, total darkness. Oh I remember things like, hiding out in the local library around the huge dictionary that unfortunately was in a big open space, so I could get a glance at the h's, for homosexuality. Or going into the file to look up and find the six books they had on the subject, only to have the lady librarian come by me and tell me that wasn't a section I should be looking at at my age. **youareafaggottom** I remember eavesdropping on other guys and hearing worse that I didn't understand but in truth knew exactly what they meant. I tried really hard to have girlfriends and dates and did but they never were right for me. But I kept trying. Mom came home from work one day telling us that a man she liked at work got fired that day. She was a bookkeeper at an exclusive mens wear store, Martins

Men's Store in the heart of downtown Louisville, but the boss had found out that the man they let go, well, he, he was different. He was queer. Mom pronounced it quare. It is like that is etched in my memory forever, because it meant that I would have to bury all of that secret away forever. Such a dark time. No wonder I "went away" for a while.

The summer after my sophomore year Mrs.French had recommended I go to a pretty high powered music camp, Meadowmount School of Music, in upstate New York. It was eight weeks long and you were required to practice five hours every weekday, four on Saturday and Sunday off. So I got to go. It was the first time to be away that long, as most camps were two weeks. It was run by the string faculty from Juilliard and I was so thrilled to go, and so nervous, because I was convinced that I would be the worst violinist there. It was the first time I felt like I was with people I could relate to, including a female cellist from near Syracuse New York, and I am happy to say we are still in touch to this day. The concerts were amazing and not only did you get assigned an incredible teacher, but they always had assistants and you could have extra lessons whenever you wanted. It was an experience I will never forget. How I loved that summer.

My senior year was my favorite high school year. I woke up from some kind of dream or something, started talking more, made lots of friends, won a few violin competitions and for the first time I wasn't being bullied. I was actually being looked upon as The Guy Most Likely to Succeed, according to the student population.

butrememberwhoyoureallyare I was having a time trying to decide what major I wanted to have. Started with being a math teacher, since I loved math, then changed it to chemistry because I loved the two years I took and I had the most awesome teacher. Actually a part of me had always wanted to be a dentist, if you can only imagine, so I was accepted as a chemistry major at Oberlin College in Ohio. That was it. I was going to do a music minor but it was science all the way.

Or so you thought

At one of my lessons in the late winter Mrs. French just randomly said

Not so random Tom   Why don't you consider doing the late audition at Juilliard in New York. I think I burst out laughing and she just looked at me and said I should talk to my parents about it. So I did. Actually the thought of going to NY again was very enticing, but there was no way I was going to get into Juilliard, no way.I had been in New York in my junior year because I was chosen to play in Carnegie Hall with the American Youth Performs. What an honor and privilege to be chosen for that. The experience was incredible. So I prepared the required repertoire and off mom and I went to New York City. We stayed at a small hotel across the street from the school. I am not sure why but mom only stayed for one day and then she flew back home and I was left to do the day of theory testing and then the actual audition. Mine was scheduled last in the day at 9pm. Of course I was a wreck but not as bad as I thought because I thought it was totally impossible for me to get in anyway. Well my audition didn't begin until after 10pm, and when I walked in there sat 10 of the worlds best violin teachers, all in a semi circle and there I was standing in front of them. I had rehearsed with an incredible pianist that I actually met at Meadowmount when I went. Sandra Rivers, who then went on to be both Perlman's pianist and Sarah Changs, was such a great person and pianist. I felt very fortunate. She told me when she saw my name on the list she signed up to accompany me. That also helped a lot with my nerves. But there they all sat. Ivan Galamian was the head of the department so he asked me what I had prepared, then he told me to start with whatever I'd like to start with, so I chose my unaccompanied Bach that I had played all year and it felt like a friend. Then they asked what modern piece I had prepared and it was a sonata by Hindemith, who was not my favorite composer, and still isn't, and it was in the annoying key of E flat major. I played part of the first movement and they stopped me. I had been warned that they would do that rather abruptly as a course of action, just to save time. Then they asked me to play the Glazounov concerto that I had come prepared with. I started at the beginning and after about three pages they stopped me and Mr. G, as he was usually called, asked me to jump to the cadenza, which I had also been warned would probably happen. Then Mr. G and Joseph Fuks started arguing whether that was required, and of course I jumped in and said I was prepared to do that, so once they stopped their power struggle they said to go ahead, and I literally played three lines and they stopped me. When they had stopped me in the beginning I was very relieved because there was a really challenging part after those first pages and thought whew, but wouldn't you know after the cadenza and argument they had me go to that part I didn't want to play and played it anyway. I had prepared about six or seven things for this audition and it looked like I was done playing. Then Mr. Galamian asked me this...

"Why do you want to come to Juilliard?" Of course I heard it with the you being really stressed, or so I thought. The only thing that came to mind was... "Why wouldn't anyone want to come to Juilliard?" Then they thanked me and I left, and flew home the next day.

About two weeks went by and since this was the late audition they let you know right away. I did it! I got into the world renowned Juilliard School! And to make it all even better, I had been accepted into the studio of the world famous Dorothy DeLay. She had been Itzakh Perlman's teacher and as the years went on she developed dozens of now extraordinary violinists who concertize to this day. Was this my lucky day? I thought...If you get into Juilliard, you don't turn it down. And so that became my life changing moment and I have never looked back. Ever. An interesting side note, my daughter Allegra actually went to Oberlin College and did her undergraduate work. Coincidence maybe?

During my senior year I had won a position in the first violins of the Louisville Orchestra, the professional orchestra in town. The conductor, Jorge Master liked to have a few of the most advanced violin students from the youth orchestra come and rehearse and play the main masterpiece concerts. I was one of three who got in, and I got to play first violin. And we got paid just like everybody else. Then at one rehearsal the maestro asked if anyone wanted to go and play in the Aspen Festival in Colorado to just come and talk to him. So I did and played again for him and he said I could go. Another feat I never thought would ever be possible. Interesting how I now live in Golden Colorado which is about three or so hours from Aspen.

So I played in the Festival Orchestra and my payment was free room and board and private lessons. For some reason I was drawn to a Japanese teacher from the Toho conservatory in Tokyo, Mr. Toshio Eto. And somehow he didn't have many students so I got to have several lessons each week. At my very first lesson with him I played the Tschaikowsky concerto, he walked over to the piano, had his back to me, and put up no music at all, and played the entire first movement accompaniment from memory without ever turning around. He turned to me when we were finished, congratulated me, then began to comment on things I would have thought he must've been able to see but actually didn't and I thought I was in the presence of something very magical. And for eight weeks every lesson was in fact just like magic. It was something to this day I will never forget, how it felt to be guided by this man. It turns out he was Shinichi Suzuki's first student when he developed his violin method for young children in Japan. Oh, and did I mention that for 47 years I studied and taught the Suzuki Method and became a trainer for teachers?

If you just look back at the last few paragraphs, you begin to see there is no such thing as this any coincidences Right?

Then it was time to get ready for my move to New York. Juilliard did not have any housing back then so it was up to the students to find their own place to live. As you can well imagine, it was really expensive, just like now to live in the city. But they had several places to recommend, so in later September we packed the car and left for my new place to reside. New York City. We drove and I remember we stayed at the Empire Hotel. We spent a few days looking and finally found a hotel, Penn Gardens Hotel, which was across the street from Penn Station and Madison Square gardens, and they had taken two floors, 5th and 6th for student housing. The rooms were really big, two bathrooms and two single beds and bunk beds. I remember my dad parked the car on the street and mom stayed with the car while we moved my things in. One of my new roommates was Bruce, a student at the Fashion Institute of Technology, and he was black. When dad and I were going back to the car for another load he told me that we should just keep that to ourselves, as he thought mom wouldn't be able to deal with it. Remember, we are from Kentucky and interestingly enough had lived through the racial riots in Kentucky in the late 1960's. I remember my dad sitting in the living room by the window with a shotgun saying he was protecting our property while the riots and marches were happening literally down the street. You see, my junior high school was the only school in the state that did not have a black student nor teacher. But that is for another time, another story. Both he and mom were quite prejudiced and so was all of the Wermuth family back then in Kentucky. But what a surprise that I wasn't, at all, and for years I was young enough not to really understand what was going on.

So, I was all moved into the Penn Gardens Hotel, with four roommates, in room 606. Done. Mom and dad were then planning to leave the city, but were very afraid they would get lost getting out of town, and since I had directed them the whole way there, I said I would get in the car and ride with them until they got to the Holland Tunnel and then get out as they went on, which is exactly what I did. I jumped out at 42nd street right by the tunnel and waved and watched the car vanish in front of me. Then I walked back to the hotel. My new home. It was exactly as I had hoped it would be...

Many Lives

So this is what freedom feels like. This is what breathing feels like. This is what happiness really feels like. This is joy.

I remember going on that adventure back to my new place, but honestly I don't remember walking. Maybe floating instead? It was a bright sunny late September day and New York was amazing. I was on 42nd street and when I finally got to Times Square I know I was smiling from ear to ear and when you are there in person it's nothing like you've ever seen on television or anything in print. There are no words really that can describe the feeling the first time you are there. And the kicker? If you go out at 2 am, which of course I did a number of times at first, it all looks exactly the same. The lights are so bright, stores are open and there are people all around it's just like the middle of the day. andthemenaretherelookingyoustraightintheeyesandyouareflus hedwithterrorandexcitement

I met with an old friend from Louisville who had also studied with Mrs. French, at 5am thank you very much, on the following Monday so that we would be at the front of the registration line at school and be able to choose the good class times before they were all taken away. There were four of us, my friend Carol who won a first violin position in the New York Philharmonic right after finishing school, and Ani and Ida Kavafian, who went the route of concert violinists, duo and amazing teachers at Curtis Institute of Music in Philadelphia. Keeping good company I'd say. They gave out numbers and we came back at 9am. At registration the last thing you do is get your student ID, and when I got mine there were things misspelled because of my southern drawl, so I made a point to be aware of my accent and worked very hard to get rid of what I could which I continued on for many years, and I do remember a time when my mom left a voicemail on one of those old small cassette answering machines, and it didn't phase me, but when a friend heard it they cracked up at her accent and it made me happy that I had worked on mine. These days it only seems to get more prominent when I am tired or have been chatting with someone else who has a southern accent. Funny how that happens.

I had three roommates. One was Bruce, the guy who was the fashion designer, Mark who was a student at the RCA electronics school, and I'm afraid I don't remember the other ones name, but he was an amazing jazz double bass player at Manhattan School of Music. They were all nice guys and we all seemed to get along well. I actually enjoyed hanging out with them more than most of the students at Juilliard because the competition at that school was fierce and that was just not my nature. Never was, never has been, never will be.

Lessons with Miss DeLay were nothing short of fantastic. *Keep paying attention Tom. Pay attention to her teaching, but also pay attention to your feelings. And please pay attention to how she listens and looks at you.*
She was so personable and made me feel welcome in her studio immediately. She had me review repertoire and learn new material. She didn't ever demonstrate for me, but she did often sit down at the piano and accompany me, which I was very familiar with since Mrs. French would do the same thing until my repertoire got so advanced I had to hire a pianist. Often it was my senior year math teacher who also had a masters in music. Go figure! But every lesson I learned that I needed to pay attention to every detail and never leave a stone unturned. The pianists we got to work with at Juilliard were usually advanced students that were of course amazing.

I also began to realize that I had many uncomfortable sexual feelings for men. I also knew that would never be accepted by my mom and dad much less anyone in my family so I kept thinking if I ignore it and find someone and get married my parents would be happy and I would be too.

And there was another very important reason why you had to get married.

During my first year at the school I found out that they hired Juilliard students for the Spoleto Festival in Italy for the summer, and I got to go. This was way before they started the american version. They paid for your trip and had us housed with a local family and gave us a weekly stipend. It was so fantastic. We played operas and ballet and concerts out in the Piazza del Duomo. It was a beautiful city and they had many superstars perform there. We did the Verdi Requiem in the Piazza and the soprano was introduced as the up and coming singer, Kathleen Battle. That was the caliber of soloists there and we had. The festival was the child of the composer Giancarlo Menotti. He was a very gentle man and had huge parties for all of us at the end of the festival. At one of them I even met the American composer Samuel Barber. In short it was the experience of a lifetime. Then I stayed for about eight weeks and traveled around and visited Austria, Switzerland, and France before I went home. We were allowed to travel back whenever we chose on an open ended ticket. I did the festival again the next summer but decided to go back home right after. I lucked out and got to stay with the same family. They were adorable. Maria cooked the most amazing fresh pasta. I would hear her in the kitchen early in the morning every day working hard on meals. One dish was better than the next. I arrived speaking no Italian at all but that didn't matter. I would say one phrase and Dario would then chatter for hours and I just smiled. Such a nice experience.

Back in New York I was now sharing an apartment with my dear friend Michael, a bassoonist that I met the first year in Italy. I hung out a lot with some friends I had met at the student housing my first year and became really close to. Her name was Jan. She was a dancer and worked and studied in the city. At one point she decided to move back to Pittsburgh and study there. We visited often and finally decided that we should get married. She had a great sense of humor, was really bright and friendly and we seemed to hit it off really quickly. And she was as kooky as one could imagine, and I say that with great affection. We actually met at the student housing I had been at in my first year there.

I had a few jobs during those years. My first one was at a good old New York coffee shop. I had to be there at 5 am to open up and get the coffee in the huge urn going. My job was to wait on the counter and three of the booths. It was a really busy location on west 72nd street, which was only six blocks from the school. I worked there for over a year, then my next job was as a waiter in a bar at Penn Station, during the rush until closing. Legal age was only eighteen back then. The tips were great because most of the after work crowd had enough to drink and I was good at conversing so they tipped really well.

butofcourseyorememberthereasonyouleftwasbecausethemana gerhadacrushonyouandtriedtodothingswithyouinhisofficeandy oufreakedout My third and last job was at a new McDonald's even closer to school. The first day I did eight hours of french fries, got my free meal when I was done, and never went back again. Just couldn't do it.

After Juilliard I needed a job so yet another coincidence happened. My friend Michael was friends with a flutist and she had a sister that was supposed to begin rehearsing and touring in the orchestra for the Canadian Opera Company, but she fell and broke her leg badly so would not be able to do the tour. I got the name of the conductor, who happened to be in New York right then, so I called him, went and played for him and he hired me on the spot. In literally three days I had a contract and a plane ticket to Toronto. We stayed at the Royal York Hotel in downtown Toronto, a really beautiful old hotel that I found out was a really desired place to stay. We were doing Mozart's opera Cosi Fan Tutti. It was a blast doing the tour. We went out for ten weeks, had a month off for the holidays then went back on the road for three months. Most of the traveling was by bus, occasionally by plane, and six nights a week we performed the 3 1/2 hour opera and would have a day off with no travel. I loved it, made a lot of great friends and saw a lot of Canada and the

United States. And even after 217 performances of that one Mozart opera I am still a fan of it and of Mozart.

The spring after the tour Jan and I got married in Clairton Pennsylvania in May of 1973. It was very unusual for me as Jan and family were Greek Orthodox Catholic, which meant we had to go for counseling with the priest before he would agree to marry us. I was not raised catholic like my dad, but Presbyterian with my mom. I guess I needed to be counseled since I wasn't the same religion. But he was very friendly and we got on well so there was no problem, except for one small detail. No music was allowed in the ceremony. No music! No exceptions. I thought that once I explained what I did in life he would take that into consideration, but no. The service was all chanted, which was very funereal. We wore wreaths on our head, marched around the church, kissed rings and I think it lasted for at least an hour and a half. I remember my cousins came and Charlie, bless his heart, had a coughing fit because the incense got so strong and thick you could hardly see anything by the end. But it was a very nice celebration.

Jan and I went back to New York the next day and had a cute apartment waiting for us on the upper west side. I did a few auditions and nothing came up for me, so we decided that I could take some decent money if I went back on the opera tour again, so I did. After the holidays Jan flew out to meet me in San Francisco and that's when I found out that I was going to be a father. Now this was what I was waiting for. This is why I had to get married. I was in heaven.

And have been ever since.

During the latter part of the tour we were going to perform in a town called Kitchener in Ontario. I had made close friends with one of the singers on the tour, and she told me the the orchestra there had been a good community orchestra and was now hiring all new principal players for the upcoming season. I knew I was not interested in doing another tour, especially with a child on the way, so when we arrived I got the conductor's phone number, gave him a call, and auditioned for him. He immediately hired me to be assistant concertmaster. Whoa! Gosh darn, another one of those coincidences just happened. I had to be there by the beginning of June as the principals would be playing at the Stratford Shakespeare Festival that summer so when I got home we started packing up and got a small uHaul, attached to the back of a Volkswagen, and headed off to Canada not knowing a thing that we were doing. I had a contract which was supposed to get us into the country. We had a cat in an empty birdcage in the back seat. Of course he was a tiger cat and he screamed the whole 8 hour trip, and by then Jan was visibly pregnant, so we must have looked like the Beverly Hillbillies. I thought we would be at Customs and Immigration for hours being searched, but when the man at the control booth looked in the car and saw my pregnant wife and a tiger cat screaming in the birdcage he just motioned us to the side and all we did was go in and get a temporary work visa for two years. I can only imagine what that border guard went home and told his family at dinner that night.

We pulled into Kitchener in the early evening, bought a newspaper, sat in a parking lot looking at the apartments for rent, made one phone call, went and saw a cute place on Hugo Crescent, signed the lease and there you have it. We were moved in by that night. I had to drive the uHaul back across the border to Niagara Falls, then back to Kitchener. Fortunately it was only a little over an hour to get to the US. The summer was great and we played operettas and chamber concerts in Stratford. It was a tiring schedule but incredibly rewarding.

The then best part comes next

On September 18th 1974 the love of my life came. My daughter was born. It had been an interesting two weeks as her mom was having false labor contractions off and on, enough so the doctor, Dr. Liang, decided that if the baby didn't come he would induce labor on the 18th. Which is exactly what happened. The labor was only a few hours, and there she was. And I was there. I was the first one who got to hold this amazing being in my arms. Funny how we had thought all along that we were having a boy, and even the doctor was convinced that was how Jan was carrying the baby. And the first thing that Jan said when she was born was "Where did she come from?" And we hadn't really decided on a name, but by the time we left the hospital we had named her Allegra after a beautiful ballerina and her middle name was Elyse, after her mom, who was Jan Elise, but insisted on the spelling change. Jan was so afraid Allegra would break, so I dressed her and carried her to the car. It was a miracle. My life has been full of many miracles...

but this was the one you have been waiting for

The first year I was also asked to fill in for an ailing teacher in the public schools. So after the holidays I got up the first morning, saw that there was at least two feet of snow, called the Board of Education because I was sure that there wouldn't be any school, and sure enough was told that we are in Canada and school does NOT get canceled, ever. So I headed out in my VW and within one block my car spun around and was heading back home, so I took that as a sign and drove right back home. My big Canadian welcome! The job was exhausting, especially since the symphony had been in full force and managing six public school classes and the symphony rehearsal and performance schedule, not to mention the newly named Stratford Festival Ensemble which comprised the principal players in the symphony, it was exhausting. I had to drive to the six different schools every day of the week, and some of them had 45 students waiting, so I learned how to tune little violins very quickly and actually loved being with the kids and teaching. But once I looked into the eyes of the students, I felt like I had come home again. Truly a wonderful feeling.

Shortly after that year I overheard a conversation at one of our symphony rehearsals and my friend Daphne Hughes was telling one of the other violinists that she was looking for a teacher to fill in at her Suzuki School in Guelph, Ontario, from March until the end of the school year. I went over to her, knowing absolutely nothing about the Suzuki Method, and asked her what was the level of the students and she said Suzuki Book 4, which were some standard concertos by Seitz and Vivaldi, as well as the Bach Concerto for two violins, and I told her I was familiar with those pieces and before you know it I had another job. I was in charge of about six young kids and didn't think I really knew much about teaching, but I loved the gig and when June came and I thanked Daphne for the experience but that I was not interested in continuing, so that was the end of it.

Or so you thought

During the following year I would ask Daphne how things were at the school and she was always so positive and enthusiastic and would let me know when there were recitals and concerts, so I went to a few. Then one day she invited me to dinner at her house and she just happened to be teaching a young girl in her living room. I remember it like it was yesterday. The girl was Jennifer Hathorn and her mom Linda was there taking notes and watching very intensely. I love it that several years later Jennifer came into my studio and stayed until she graduated from high school.

So what did you think Tom?

That was it. When I went home later that night I called her and told her that I really was interested and would she consider me teaching at the school the next year. She said she knew all along that I was the right person for this way of teaching and encouraged me to attend a Suzuki Institute during the summer. Talk about coincidences, the workshop was at the University of Louisville, and they were having the very first official teacher training course taught by Kay Collier Slone at the University, having taught these classes many times at other locations. This was, at the risk of being dramatic, life changing for me. I went into the first class thinking, I studied at Juilliard with Dorothy DeLay, so what is this woman going to be able to tell me that I don't know already? When I think back on this it really makes me laugh because the truth is I knew nothing about teaching nor about young children, other than I had already started teaching my own daughter Allegra. The course was wonderful and I left there feeling like I had found out something really extraordinary about myself. The sheer grounding I felt during these classes were worth the price alone.

So it begins, right? A life long dream for you.

I started teaching at the Suzuki String School of Guelph in the fall and stayed there for about ten years.

But something is in your way. And you know exactly what it is, so isn't it time to be honest and truthful about that?

I came home one day and something snapped. Me. I can remember it was a beautiful fall day. I got angry about something, which wasn't necessarily in my nature, and I picked up a dining room chair and just hit the floor with it. And I did it again, and again and got more heavy handed and finally the legs broke off. Then I picked up another chair and did the same thing. I had never felt this good in my life. I could feel the anger literally flying out of me. Later that day my wife Jan confronted me and I said "If it weren't for you I would be gay". And she said she knew. She knew, We separated shortly after that and then it wasn't too long before we were divorced. Fortunately I feel we had a very balanced daughter and we lived in very close proximity and Jan was always so great about the importance of me being with Allegra .But needless to say no matter what the circumstances divorce is really challenging especially when there is a child involved. Both Jan and I felt strongly that we each had a really strong relationship with our daughter individually which we felt made a big difference.

A few years later Jan remarried and they decided to move to Albany NY.

I was heartbroken. Right now that period of time is somewhat of a blur to me. I do remember one time when I went to pick up Allegra and we ended up back in Kitchener, and when I had to take her home we drove the eight hours to get there, and I turned around and drove the eight hours back. It was really awful.

This was a huge turning point for me. I had been spending my summers teaching at various Suzuki Institutes in north america. My first one was Kingston Ontario, then Ithaca NY, Washington DC, Columbus OH, and did workshops in Miami. Allegra went everywhere with me and studied with some of the most amazing teachers I have ever known. And for me it was truly a blessing that we got to spend such quality time together.

And time for a change, isn't it?

One summer at the Ithaca Institute one of the usual faculty members had passed away unfortunately, so the new hire was a man from the Chicago area that I had heard about earlier that summer. The director of the Western Springs School of Talent Education, Edward Kreitman, was the new faculty member and we connected immediately. By the end of that season, 1988-89, I resigned from the symphony and moved to Illinois. The school was in fact in Western Springs, which is an absolutely adorable town I affectionately have always referred to as the 'Leave it to Beaver' town, for those of you in my generation that know about that television show. The houses were beautiful, kids can easily and safely ride their bike to grade school or middle school and to the library. The downtown is about four or five blocks long with shops, small grocers, and and amazing bakery.

I spent the next 32 years of my life teaching at the school. I was basically in charge of the advanced level violinists. To this day I am very proud of the studio I maintained for all of those years, and I am still in touch with many of my former students who have gone on to have amazing careers as soloists, chamber musicians, teachers and symphony players. My students have attended The Curtis Instituter of Music, Juilliard, New England Conservatory, The Cleveland Institute of Music, as well as many Universities and Colleges. As well as maintaining a yearly class of nearly thirty students, I developed my beloved violin choir. It was initially named The Advanced Violin Ensemble from the Western Springs School of Talent Education, which was a mouthful, so we decided to change it and came up with Cantabile. For us musicians that is a lovely word and means in a singing manner. When the group was playing at a huge office building in downtown Chicago at Christmas time we overheard a gentleman reading the sign and pronouncing it 'can't - a - bile', so we immediately decided to change the name and came up with Consort, which is a group of like instruments, and instead of locating the group in Western Springs, we decided on the Chicago Consort. And I am very proud to say that to this day that group is thriving and traveling and playing incredibly.

Consort has traveled to many places in the world, Italy, London, Paris, Austria and Iceland as well as many other places. We have played in the most beautiful cathedrals in Peru, Greece, France and England, and during a very brief period of time when the US and Cuba were getting along, we were able to travel there for three concerts. We have been chosen to play several times on the International Ensembles Concert at the Suzuki of the Americas Conference. I loved working with this group every Wednesday night for all the years I was at the school. We have produced several compact discs, the last one being 'Contrasts'. The opening solo is my daughter playing an arrangement of 'Mi Mancherai', which means I will miss you. I have such fondness for this as the week we recorded it I found out that I was going to be a grandfather. Every time I listen to it it seems to get harder and harder to hold the tears back. These CD's are available today from WSSTE.com.

Since I had moved to the midwest I was getting asked to join other Suzuki Institutes and teach. I had become a teacher trainer so my work was pretty much divided between teaching kids and teachers. One of the workshops was in Stevens Point WI which was only about five hours away from home. During one of those weeks there I went to lunch with some friends and they began to talk about people who could see auras. I was really fascinated by their conversation

Go ahead and say it Tom
And I suddenly realized that I could see those auras too
And you always have been seeing them   Ever since you were born

When you have a realization like that it's sometimes like a dam breaking loose and everything suddenly came flooding to me. After lunch we went back to teaching and when I was done I started walking to my dormitory room and passed a mom and a really cute little child. They smiled and waved, and once they were past me I had a vision of them in front of me, although they were way behind me, and I couldn't see their actual bodies, but I was seeing colors and waves and movement around them. Boy did I head right back to my room. I fretted about this, oh, pretty much for the next 48 hours then I finally decided to approach a teacher I was very friendly and comfortable with and had known from several different Institutes. When I got brave enough to finally tell him, he looked at me and the only thing I remember him saying was that I had to make a choice immediately to either put it back away, far far away, or keep it in my realm of consciousness and start doing something about it. Thank you, Craig, for just being you.

Before long there was an Expo in Chicago called Whole Life Expo and a good friend asked me if I wanted to go with her. So a few of us went to the expo and I wandered away from them because they wanted to go to see a certain exhibit, and I had seen that Barbara Brennan was there giving a lecture. I went in and sat at the back and there was literature on all the chairs for her school of healing. My first reaction is that it was just going to be a sales pitch for her school. Which it absolutely was not. Her lecture was Matters of the Heart. She started the session with a meditation and it was not only an experience I had not had, it was an experience I will truly never forget. At one point I thought I was on the ceiling floating. I had, as a child, had a few small experiences with prayer in the church that my mom and I would go to, but nothing like this. There must have been a few hundred people at this lecture and the power of that many people meditating was truly amazing.
Just keep paying attention to this.

So one thing led to another and within a short while I had enrolled in the healing schools four year program. The school was then located in upstate New York and starting in October you would attend for a week every other month. I was very fortunate to have many supportive people for this in my life and a dear teacher friend and my daughter would come in from out of town and teach my students for me when I was gone, so it worked out that they never had to go without their lessons. My mom had moved to Oak Park, where I was living, a year before and she was also very curious and supportive of my new adventure.

My arrival at the school was so fascinating. When I was standing in line to check into the hotel where the classes were being held I observed many people hugging and smiling and the energy was quite palpable and immediately felt really wonderful. At one point I overheard a student who was going into her second year say to one of her friends that she had never cried so much the previous year and wondered if it would be like that again this year and my first thought was oh my, what did I just get myself into. Also back in Chicago I had a really good healer friend that had actually graduated a few years before, and when I first went to her when I was considering going to the school and asked her what it was like and all she ever said to me is "it's a pressure cooker". Whoa! And it was, in so many wonderful ways.

Well, going to BBSH is everything and more. The faculty is unequaled anywhere I have ever been in any possible setting. The kindness and love follows you around one hundred percent. You go there thinking oh how cool, I'm going to learn these great hands on healing techniques, which is true, but I believe the one of the basic premises that Barbara holds is that you cannot be of true service in this world unless you can go into the depths of your soul and clear everything you need to. Every time I would arrive back home after a week of training my energy field would be so open that sometimes it was really hard to drop right back into my life.

Then it finally happened

During the very first week of classes I had one of my greatest experiences. I clearly remember sitting on the floor and we had broken into groups and the subject was spirit guides. Do we have guides? As the lecture went on and we were chatting and relating, all of a sudden I remembered. I had an energy guide when I was young. His name was Rankso.

And I have been by your side for the last forty some years never leaving your side even if you didn't see nor remember me Welcome home Tom Your violin had kept us together for oh so many wonderful years

I was finally at home and in that instant I saw my guide sitting beside me absolutely glowing with the most intense gold light I could have ever imagined, and I did remember that he had always been by my side. I was in awe of this next path I was going to be on, and have never looked back. I realize once you are on the path of awakening you never go back, only forward, sometimes really fast, sometimes at a snail's pace, and even though you might feel like you have halted or are moving backwards, you are in fact always moving forward. It is such an amazing journey. Sometimes I even think that before I went to the school I cannot even really remember what my life was like. Ever since graduating I feel a light in me that has never and can never be diminished. Ever. I am so very grateful that I attended and began the journey of going back to remembering who I really am.

After I did the four year diploma I decided to take a year off and work in the field. By the time the year ended I had over twenty clients. In the years since I graduated I maintained many of these clients and have been very grateful to be able to do the work. After a year off I went back to the school to do their advanced training. My intention was to stay for another two years and possibly go into the teachers program to teach at the school, but something made me change my mind. I loved doing the advanced training and in one of our last classes Barbara was there, we worked on doing stand up healing work instead of on the table, which really made me think about my teaching. At one point Barbara asked me what was the music I was hearing in my head, and I thought what a difference between then and my first year at the school. At first I would find myself diverting my path when I would see her, feeling a huge fear that she would see who I really was. By the time I was in the advanced class, when she asked me about myself I felt the most intense gratitude well up inside of me, not only did she care to know me, but it was the first time I really talked about my life, my music, my teaching, and I finally realized that what was going on in my own backyard was enough for me. Because for the first time in my life, I felt like I was enough.

There are only two things I wish to reflect on during this last time I spent in Illinois. The next, and clearly one of the most important things was that I met my current partner Nick. If someone asked me to tell you about him in one sentence, I would have to say that I finally met the most genuine and kindest person I have ever known. We met in September of 2006 and once again I have never looked back. He is low keyed, low energy, loves to travel and fits in with my family perfectly. Who says I am not the luckiest man in the world.

Betty died. That soul finally found peace.

Mom passed on January 3rd 2015. I have every bit of confidence that she does rest in peace. And I will always be grateful that she was in my life. I have conversations with her regularly and appreciate her guidance and her looking after me. As difficult as I felt she was, I will always be grateful that she was such a profound teacher for me. Actually the perfect teacher for me.

The other thing, or event I should say that happened was, in the blink of an eye, my life physically changed forever. I do not have the amount of time to really elaborate, but I feel that I have to share just a bit of my story. In March of 2017 I was suffering from a really bad upper respiratory infection and I just couldn't seem to knock it. It had started in November of the previous year right before Thanksgiving and I can remember the day I caught the virus. I can remember the moment and unfortunately the student that gave it to me. My doctor had given me two different antibiotics that just didn't seem to work. I was scheduled to leave on St. Patrick's Day to teach a workshop at the University of Hartford so I either needed to get a handle on it or cancel, which I did not want to do. So I made another appointment and my doctor was not available. The wonderful doctor that had looked after my mom for many years was available at the same clinic so I went to see her. After she checked me over she said the words that have haunted me ever since. She said "I'm going to give you Levaquin. Is that okay?"

Is that okay   Is that okay   Is that okay   How odd
How that haunts me to this day. I said of course it's okay, why shouldn't it be? I reminded her that she had given it to

my mom in her 80's for bronchitis so why wouldn't it be fine for me? I went to the pharmacy and then home and took that first dose. I should have recognized something was off when I had one of the worst nightmares I have ever had that very night. But I did not see a connection. This was a Monday. I took my two doses the next day and had another nightmare. By Wednesday I was finally beginning to feel that I was starting to get better, but again woke myself and Nick up screaming. So on Friday morning I was up early and on my way to the airport. I decided to be really good and save money and park in the remote lot at OHare airport, and had about a three block walk to catch the train into the terminal. If anyone ever tells you that the American Airlines corridor in Terminal 3 is a long one, wouldn't you know that I was at the last gate on the concourse. The whole time I was walking I kept thinking I should have worn other shoes, not these old ones, but I knew they had a mountain of snow in Hartford and once again thought I was being smart. I arrived and as the day went on I started teaching and by the evening I was in a fair amount of pain but in typical Tom fashion I just kept teaching and trudging on, but was having a really difficult time walking. That night I had another nightmare and was beating myself up thinking that any of the people staying at the hotel probably was wondering what was happening as I woke myself up screaming. When I got up I fell because I lost my balance. I could go on and on but just suffice to say something was wrong. But again in typical Tom fashion, I was blaming myself the whole time that it was my fault about the shoes and just took ibuprofen and iced my now swollen and turning black and purple feet.

My trip back home was horrible, as I think I must've passed out when the plane landed and was trying to get my cane that a dear friend had given me out of the storage compartment above my seat. I woke up when a very sweet woman asked me if I was okay and she got it for me. Since I had parked at the remote lot, by the time I got from the plane down the corridor onto the shuttle train and then walked the blocks to my car it took two and a half hours. Little did I know that the entire weekend my tendons had been tearing. But who would have known?

Like a good boy of course I had been faithfully taking the antibiotic and the day I took the very last dose I found out that there were a few cases of people having tendon issues with Levaquin. When one of my students' mom put me onto it I went home and realized that is exactly what had happened to me. I made a doctor's appointment with my regular doctor and I can remember the look on his face when he saw my achilles tendons. They were ruptured. Then began the long saga of doctors, casts, boots and medications, not to mention more reactions. Turns out it can wreak havoc with blood pressure, cause permanent nerve damage, I have a blob in the center of my left eye that my doctors agree are due to the drug.

I have decided this story could go on and on for quite awhile. Maybe that's a tale for another time. I am proud that ten days after I was let out of the cast and boots I took my Consort on tour to Cuba, wheelchair and all, and did three concerts. It might not have been the wisest decision in my life, but I did it because I felt that I was devoted to my group.
wimp

But that was the beginning of the end of your touring with your beloved group   Something was shifting

I have learned so much from this injury. The most important thing is that not everyone would have been so kind to me like Nick has been. He has never complained to me, and has been there every possible step of the way with me, and for that I will always be eternally grateful. It takes a very strong being to be able to go through with someone what he has gone through as I have traveled this path, and his love and care and devotion has been astounding and never failing. I really wonder if I would have survived this trauma if he hadn't been by my side. Also my daughter has been the best cheerleader that anyone could ever want. She has always made me feel that I could do anything that I want and that alone has been a Godsend. My beautiful granddaughter has an amazing was of knowing when something is wrong and needs attention. Often out of the blue I would get a text from her full of joyous emoji. It always makes me feel good. I had many friends and students that really helped me on the way, especially my students and their parents, but I have to say that not everybody has the strength to be able to tolerate when people are having struggle as big as this, so I began to realize that I needed to be thinking about my future. As far as my health goes, it is very hard to be in pain 24/7 for what is now over 2000 days. It is wearisome. But the lessons I have learned have been monumental. Slowing down, being more present, and not focusing on myself have been the biggest. It's really hard when your pain scale is from about a 3 to an 8 on any given day. But pain is a very interesting thing. The less you focus on it and the more you focus on being happy and content and joyful you don't notice it so much. And the more you feel love in your heart the better anything is.

We toured Iceland and Sweden in June of 2019 and I announced privately to the powers that be that it would be my last tour. While I love traveling and would love to continue, I need to be able to do it at my own leisure and not with any strict time constraint. I have loved touring and as you know I love my ensemble, but another thing I have learned is that you have to love yourself too. As my dear mentor Barbara Brennan said, you will never be of service to anyone else if you don't take care of yourself first. The last time we had gone to Colorado to visit my daughter and granddaughter I remember texting her at a prescribed pick up time where we were staying and told her it was the first time in all the years of coming to visit that I did not have any altitude problems, she texted back that maybe Nick and I should consider moving here.

And a really good seed was planted

So at that same announcement I actually continued that I would be retiring from the school in June of 2021 and we would be moving to Colorado.

Which is exactly what happened.

Of course I don't need to tell anyone in this world we live in that a pandemic happened in the meantime. But it did not stop the plan from happening. We found an apartment in Golden Colorado, where my daughter and granddaughter live, unseen by us, but when the leasing agent sent us a picture of what our view would be like off of our balcony, that was it. Done deal.

And you have never been happier and have not even thought about looking back once   One of the best decisions of your life Tom and you know it   Don't look back   Don't be afraid of your future   You still have work to do and missions to accomplish   There is no such thing as time for you have all of the time you will ever need   It is all perfectly planned

Conscience

soyouwroteabookwhothefuckcaresnobodywillreaditandifanybodyd
oestheywontfinishitabunchofdrivellookintoyourowneyesandyouwon'tfi
ndanydepthmuchlessanythingreallyworthsayingBettscalledyouaweakli
ngmaybeshewasrightyouhaveneverbeenabletostanduptoanyoneandthe
nyouspendsomuchofyourlifeapologizingheyallyouneedtodoisapologizef
orbeinghereforbeingevenbeingalivemaybeCarolwasrightandyoushouldn'tb
ehereafterallyourmomwasn'tsupposedtobeabletohavechildrenandjustlookwhatha
ppenedtalkaboutanaccidentyouspendallofthistimeoverseventyyearsjusgoingthroughthem
otionsoflifeanyonecanlearntoplayaninstrumentdidyoueverwonderwhyyoudidn'tauditionfo
rotherorchestrastotryandraiseyourlevelofcoursenotyouweretoochickenormaybeyoureallyknewyo
ujustweren'tgoodenougheverydayyougetupandyouthinkifyoufakebeinghappysomethinggoodwillh
appenbutthetruthisyoujustaren'tgoodenoughforabetterlifeyouthinkyouloveyourlifebutthetruthisyou
justhaven'tdoneanythingatallatleastnotanythingworthwhileallofthosekidsyoutaughtmuchlessthoseteacherstheycouldbestud
yingwithanybodyelseandhavedonebetterthanwithyoujustgetoveryourselfyoukeptwonderingyourwholechildhoodifyourmomwasmadetyouofcourseshewashaing
nnonwho'snotonlyweakbutprettystupidaswellifyouhadjustappliedyourselfwhoareyouereyouangeryou

and now the lesson is   you have a choice   you can
continue to listen to that voice inside your head   the one that
has been there forever   shaming you   scaring you
intimidating you   you have a choice Tom   you always have
time to start trusting and listening to you gut   you have
much more love to give than any voice can ever take away
from you   you are finally remembering who you really are

Coda

As a musician I would be lying if I told you that we aren't happy and relieved when we finally turn the page of a long work, maybe a ballet or opera or even a Strauss waltz, and see the word Coda. Mind you I absolutely love to play those works, and I have always been fond of Strauss waltzes even though I played viola for so many years, which means endless pah pah coming after the oomph, but a very lengthy work can actually be physically exhausting to play. You might even be doing a run for a week or so as well. Another word, particularly in ballets instead of coda they often use Gallop which personally cracks me up. You see when you are playing these you are most likely under the stage in the orchestra pit, and those dancers with the wooden blocks in their toe shoes actually sound like ponies on the stage right above you. But suffice to say that we all love it when the end of the work is near. Besides, nothing is ever really 'over'.

Codas often reflect melodies, sometimes in a variation form, that are heard during the work, or they bring back a melody from the very opening. That brings me back to my thoughts on memory at the beginning of this tale. I do realize that memory is in the mind of the beholder. Often when I think of stories from my childhood I think to myself do I remember that because I've heard a parent or sibling or a good friend tell the story many times? Or am I actually remembering it truly. I have tried to be very careful in my writing of events and can say my stories are completely truthful. I may have experienced regression therapies to remember some but otherwise they are right from my souls memory.

Another thing I find fascinating about a Coda is that very subtly the composer will introduce another melody, or perhaps a variation of one in the work, or maybe they have a way of triggering a thought or emotion in us. These are some of the wonderful puzzles we musicians have going though our minds when we are performing. I even know there are composers who take that thought or melody into the next work that they write. Perhaps it's guidance that is urging us to move in that direction.

Hmmm

I found it very interesting while I was writing that I would often reflect on the story at hand and my mind would move into thinking about how much of my past life or lives has had a direct effect on what I might have just written. That occurred to me more than once I have to say. In fact as I think about it right now *Food for another tale perhaps* I know from past experiences that our past lives do often cause a new effect in a current lifetime situation. Who knows. But it does feel right.

I have been very fortunate to have lived a very full and meaningful life. I am grateful every day as my thoughts float through my mind. I have traveled to all fifty states in the US, all of the Canadian provinces, mainstream Europe, China, Australia, Scandinavia and Peru. I've climbed the Great Wall of China, the Acropolis and Machu Picchu, which was clearly on my bucket list for my entire life. My daughter and I climbed the Leaning Tower of Pisa the final summer that it was open to the public, and after climbing I am certain they made the right decision to close. It was pretty scary. I've taught in Sweden, France, the UK as well as most of the states. I have been able to swim in Iceland's Blue Lagoon and wandered through the Mammoth Caves in Kentucky. I have played with the most incredible musicians and under the batons of many wonderful conductors. *And you have worked very hard your entire life to deserve this   You have never been one to give up*

Right now I feel like I am able to experience this time in my life to the fullest. It has been a dream for a long time to live here in Golden Colorado, and being only minutes away from my daughter and granddaughter is the icing on the cake. There are very few moments that go by when I don't have a big smile on my face and I thank the Universe every day for my good fortune. When I am driving, maybe even getting lost, I am in awe of the beauty that surrounds me here in this state. It is so interesting to me that everyone wants to go to Europe, Asia, South America, or Africa, but the truth is that right here in our very own homeland are some of the most incredibly beautiful places to see. I don't think I really ever appreciated that until I actually moved from the midwest to Colorado. I look forward to what will come. I know everything happens for a reason and accept that, even though there are events that make me wonder if that's true, but I am open to discoveries of any and all kinds.

My last thoughts here are for the moms, dads, brothers, sisters and teachers of our children to keep an open mind to everything. Be the role model you want your child to be. Be the role model you want your students to be. If you are tense and angry, they will be too. You can't expect them to do as you say if it doesn't reflect what you do yourself. One of the best skills we worked on at the healing school was listening. I learned so much about myself and others by helping myself to quiet my mind so that I could really hear what was being said to me. As time continues I realize I am not always just hearing with my ears. Our eyes and bodies can hear if our mind is quiet. Everybody has a story that deserves to be heard. Every student I have taught has had valuable life experiences for me to understand. Don't let their age, especially the younger ones influence what you think they are telling you. Just look into their eyes. They tell all and tell the truth. Please, never, never assume anything. Do not be afraid of their answer to your questions. Their answers may not always be what you want to hear, but what you have to say may not be exactly what the other needs either. If you honestly are there for your children they will honestly come to you in their time of need. Be willing to look inward as you spend time with your kids, students, your own parents and relatives, and learn how to center and quiet yourselves. You just might be surprised that the story you thought you were going to hear actually went in a completely different direction that you expected. This is the beauty of individuality. You will teach others that you are truly willing to be there for them, and it's not about you, it's about them. Please keep remembering that this is not a dress rehearsal, it's life, and there are no mistakes nor failures. Just lessons. We are always teaching and learning simultaneously. And, this is a big one, you will never really know what goes on behind the closed doors of the person in front of you, whether they are young or old. So please be as mindful as you can be.

And lastly, if you're being told about an imaginary friend, no matter who is telling you, listen really carefully with your eyes, ears, body and mind. You might just begin to know not only more about others, but you'll begin to know more of who you really truly are.

Thomas Wermuth
Namaste

Acknowledgements

I am blessed to have the most loving and supportive family, my daughter, granddaughter and partner Nick. They have encouraged me to write and develop this newly found talent. The back cover of the book is a photo of a large charcoal drawing of myself leading a concert in Chicago's Symphony Center. The work was a gift to me drawn by my student Aura Evans when she graduated from our school. I feel myself in this more than any other image of myself and will treasure this drawing forever.

About the Author

Journey along with Thomas Wermuth from his earthly beginnings in Kentucky through a very challenging childhood, learning to play an instrument that led him to the Juilliard School. From his life in New York to living in Canada performing in orchestral, chamber and solo events Thomas starts his professional musical career that takes him to many corners of the world. As a widely sought after teacher in Chicago as well as a trainer for other new teachers he also attended the Barbara Brennan School of Healing and developed a very successful healing practice. Read how his personal healing and growth has now taken him to Golden Colorado to spend this next part of his life with his family.

CPSIA information can be obtained
at www.ICGtesting.com
Printed in the USA
LVHW072345100223
739201LV00011B/358

9 781915 904096